AP
Associated Press

Reporting Handbook

Other titles in the Associated Press Series

Associated Press Broadcast News Handbook by Brad Kalbfeld

Associated Press Guide to Photojournalism, Second Edition, by Brian Horton

Associated Press Sports Writing Handbook by Steve Wilstein

AP Associated Press

Reporting Handbook

Jerry Schwartz

McGraw-Hill

New York   Chicago   San Francisco   Lisbon
London   Madrid   Mexico City   Milan   New Delhi
San Juan   Seoul   Singapore   Sydney   Toronto

McGraw-Hill

A Division of The **McGraw·Hill** *Companies*

1 2 3 4 5 6 7 8 9 0   DOC/DOC   0 9 8 7 6 5 4 3 2 1

ISBN 0-07-137217-2

This book was set in Stempel Garamond by North Market Street Graphics.

Printed and bound by R.R. Donnelley & Sons Company.

This publication is designed to provide accurate and authoritative information in regard to the subject matter covered. It is sold with the understanding that the publisher is not engaged in rendering legal, accounting, or other professional service. If legal advice or other expert assistance is required, the services of a competent professional person should be sought.
—*From a declaration of principles jointly adopted by a committee of the American Bar Association and a committee of publishers.*

 This book is printed on recycled, acid-free paper containing a minimum of 50% recycled de-inked fiber.

McGraw-Hill books are available at special quantity discounts to use as premiums and sales promotions, or for use in corporate training programs. For more information, please write to the Director of Special Sales, Professional Publishing, McGraw-Hill, Two Penn Plaza, New York, NY 10121-2298. Or contact your local bookstore.

Contents

Contents

Contents

Acknowledgments

The joy of writing this book was working with the tremendously talented people who are its focus—the men and women who took the time to share their stories and their methods. Their names often are cloaked in wire-service obscurity. They should not be.

The frustration of writing this book was the impossibility of including the many other fine reporters who produce great stories for the AP every day, sometimes between running the broadcast wire and writing high school basketball roundups. Yes, this is every bit as hard as it sounds.

The agony of writing this book was—well, writing this book. My family put up with much whining; for that and so much else, my unending gratitude and everlasting love to Nina Ovryn and to Danny, Joshua, and Benjamin.

AP
Associated Press

Reporting Handbook

Introduction

George Esper just stood there.

He wanted this story. He wanted every story, but this was the story he wanted now. He had gone to Vietnam, had covered the war on the battlefield, had gained fame and admiration within the profession as the last American reporter to leave Saigon after the communists swept in. Now, two decades later, he was covering the war on the home front; 20 years had passed since the shootings of four Kent State students by National Guardsmen, and Esper was writing about Vietnam again.

He planned to interview the mothers of all four of the slain students for a sidebar—what were their thoughts after all these years? He reached three of the women, but he had no phone number for the last one, just a street address. So he got into his car and drove an hour through a ferocious snowstorm.

He knocked on the door at 7 a.m. Florence Schroeder answered it.

My name is George Esper, he said, and I'm from The Associated Press.

"She just kind of waved me off, and she said, 'We're not giving any interviews.' Just like that," Esper recalls. "I didn't really push her. On the other hand, I didn't turn around and leave. I just kind of stood there, wet with snow, dripping wet and cold, and I think she kind of took pity on me."

"Come on in," she said. And after some small talk, Florence Schroeder talked for two hours about her son, dead 20 years. "At the end of the interview, she told me she never thought she would go that deep into her heart again," Esper says. "But she did it."

Why did she do it? Esper has some theories. Maybe it was just a matter of pity—a sodden reporter showed up at her door, and she didn't have the heart to turn him away. Maybe it was Esper's obvious sympathy; after a lifetime of covering tragedies, he had not become callous. Or maybe she was just ready to talk, and Esper was the one who knocked on the door.

But the fact is, she did talk, and this was no fluke. For more than four decades, Esper always got the story—sometimes through cunning, sometimes through empathy, always through persistence and tenacity.

This is a book about people like George Esper, about how they do the job they do. This is a book about reporting—not writing, though there are many outstanding examples of it in these pages. As AP writing guru Rene J. Cappon says, "Reporting is the essence of good writing." Without the raw material of reportage, a story is just a collection of pretty words, signifying nothing.

From the instant it was created in 1848, the AP's purpose was to report the news. AP reporters covered the 1848 presidential campaign, announcing the election of James Knox Polk. An AP correspondent, Mark Kellogg, rode with George Armstrong Custer at the Little Big Horn and suffered the same unhappy fate as Custer's men. In the 24 hours after the San Francisco earthquake of 1906, the AP's office there transmitted 21,300 words about the devastation.

The story of Mahatma Gandhi has often been told: how the Hindu leader was arrested by the British in 1932, spent months in prison, and finally was released under great secrecy. He was let go after midnight and driven to a distant railroad station, where he dragged his belongings onto the platform. There, in the darkness, he recognized Jim Mills, an AP reporter who had chronicled Gandhi's efforts to gain independence for India. Somehow, Mills alone had learned of Gandhi's release.

"I suppose when I go to the Hereafter and stand at the Golden Gate," Gandhi said, "the first person I shall meet will be a correspondent of The Associated Press."

News gathering is so ingrained in the AP's culture that for some, reporting seems like breathing—necessary, but not all that complicated or interesting.

"Hmm, a guide to reporting," mused Special Correspondent Mort Rosenblum.

"A. Get on a plane.

"B. Tell the desk all the stuff you see.

"C. Have a double expense-account whiskey when you see the result.

"So what are the other 70,000 words going to be?"

But this business of getting the news IS interesting, and there is something to be learned from how various reporters go about it. It's not as simple as compiling a list of reporting do's and don'ts—do this and this and this and you'll be a good reporter. "There are no rules," says Special Correspondent Helen O'Neill, and though this has its limits—you don't, for example, commit felonies to get a story—the point

is well taken. Reporters make up their own rules as they go along, depending on their own strengths—and weaknesses.

In the movies, reporters are urbane and sardonic, barely breaking a sweat to make the front page. In reality, there's a lot of sweat, and the process can be messy or tedious. Mitchell Landsberg, a longtime AP reporter who went on to The Los Angeles Times, once said that his interviewing technique consisted of stumbling and stuttering so much that his subject finally took pity on him and told him everything he needed to know. He was exaggerating, but there are successful reporters who struggle through interviews, or don't know their way around a database, or would be boggled by a complicated investigation.

Their strengths, though, carry them through. And the ways in which they use their strengths—interviewing techniques, source development, organizational skills—are all things that can be emulated.

We can't all be Helen O'Neill, writing extraordinary, intimate profiles, but perhaps we can pick up some ideas on how to get close to an interview subject. We can't all be Marc Humbert, breaking political stories every day, but the way he handles his sources might be instructive. We can't all be Ted Anthony, inhaling life and drawing ideas from it as if it were one big story factory. But if we could see the world through his eyes for a moment, vistas of possible stories might open up to us.

Ask George Esper about his strengths, and the first thing he will tell you is that he is very curious. "Even my family always says to me, 'Geez, you ask so many questions.' Even when I'm not reporting, I'm interested. I may meet a husband and wife or girlfriend and boyfriend, and I'll ask, 'How did you meet?' I kind of go into their history, where they went to school, what they majored in."

To be a good reporter, "you have to enjoy it. It has to be fun," Esper says. What's fun? "Finding out about people." He always has another question. Too many reporters will "ask a question and they'll get an answer and there's no follow-up, to probe a little deeper."

Esper's other great strength is persistence. When a youth committed suicide in Maine, Esper called the young man's father seven days in a row, pursuing an interview. "You don't want to be obnoxious and you don't want to stalk people, but I think persistence pays off."

When he talked to the boy's father, he was deeply solicitous. He is just as tenacious, if less solicitous, when he is covering a war.

"Not that I dislike the military, but I think they're fair game and I think the public is entitled to know what is happening in a war, be it the Vietnam War or the Gulf War, because there's taxpayers' money involved, people's lives involved," he says. "If I don't get an answer, I keep hammering away: 'When are you going to know?' 'Why don't you know?'

"Sometimes I even use threats. I don't mean physical threats or anything—saying, in effect, look, if you can't give me this, I'll call your boss or I'll call the Pentagon or I'll write a story saying you're trying to cover this up. This actually happened in Vietnam many times, where you just keep pounding them with questions: 'Why don't you know? You should know this. I know you know it.' "

Others, he says, assume that people won't talk to them or that they can't get information from the military. "They give up too easily. I say, never give up."

Some of his biggest Vietnam stories, he says, were easier than they looked. There was the story of a bomber pilot who refused to fly.

"All I saw was an incoming story from Omaha, Neb., the headquarters of the Strategic Air Command, saying Capt. Michael Heck was being court-martialed after refusing to fly B-52 missions. That's all we had. And I looked at this, and I said, 'Gee, if we could interview this guy, what a story!'"

He knew he would not be able to go to an air base to interview Heck. But he could use the military telephone lines, and he could use his knowledge of the military to track Heck down. There were three B-52 bases; he called the nearest one, in Thailand.

"It was this simple: I said 'base locator.' I got the base locator. And I said, 'Could I speak to Capt. Michael Heck?' And within 30 seconds I was speaking to Capt. Michael Heck."

Esper had tracked Heck down to an officer's club bar in U Tapao, Thailand. He was rewarded with "a tremendous interview. He said, 'I just got tired of killing women and children.' And this is why he had stopped flying. This guy was no kook; he had flown like a hundred missions, he was heavily decorated, and in many ways he was a hero. And suddenly, he stops flying.

"Well, the rest of the press corps was really furious with me. They said, 'You've got to tell us where this Capt. Heck is. . . .' They assumed that I had either flown into a Thailand air base and interviewed him or that I was hiding him out in Saigon. They never guessed what I thought was obvious.

"I simply phoned him."

Of course, by then Heck wasn't talking to any other reporters anyway. Esper had suggested it was best to keep quiet. "Unfortunately, there are some people you just can't trust," he told the young officer.

Oh, yes. It's worth noting that besides curiosity and tenacity, George Esper possesses a fine and well-sharpened appetite for competition.

1 Anatomy of a Story: Covering a Plane Crash

The televisions were on in the AP's Los Angeles bureau; they're always on, just in case a station is reporting something that the AP doesn't have or in case the helicopters that scour the sky over southern California happen on some news. " 'Breaking news' labels pop up all the time, and it's usually just a car wreck," says John Antczak, the veteran editor and reporter who was the bureau's supervisor in the late afternoon of the last day of January 2000.

Suddenly, something on KABC caught Antczak's eye, and he turned up the sound. The Federal Aviation Administration had reported a plane crash. He listened carefully. "It was complete, it was attributed, there weren't any weasel words like 'we think' or 'we're checking this out,' " he says. There was enough there to file a bulletin series.

It was 4:53 p.m.

AM-CA—Airliner Crash, 28

LOS ANGELES (AP)—An Alaska Airlines Boeing 737 crashed Monday northwest of Los Angeles on a flight from Puerto Vallarta, Mexico, KABC-TV reported.
MORE

AM-CA—Airliner Crash, 1st Add, 34

KABC said the aircraft went down 27 miles northwest of Los Angeles International Airport.
KCAL-TV reported from a helicopter off Point Mugu that there was a large slick in the water.

Antczak looked around. If there ever was a good time of day for a plane crash—and there isn't—this was it. He had a full staff; most of the day shift was still there, and the evening shift was just arriving. "You can write, file the wire, and yell instructions to people at the same time," he says. "Yelling doesn't sound high-tech, but a loud voice is an effective way to get everyone in a very large office to drop what they're doing and get aboard the big story immediately."

The first priority: reach the FAA and confirm the television report. Antczak told Louinn Lota and John Rogers to work the phones; the FAA Pacific regional office had moved to Seattle from Los Angeles, and Antczak knew from experience that it would be difficult to reach.

In the same breath he told staffers Ken Peters and Cindy Webb to drive toward the crash. Peters is the bureau's sports editor. "As soon as I yelled that there had been an air crash, he was already out of his chair and ready to go," Antczak says. "That's the kind of reaction I want."

The problem was, Antczak didn't know exactly where they were going; the first report didn't give a precise location of the crash, and in fact, the first reports were off by more than 10 miles.

"Just keep driving," he told them.

Antczak, like others in the Los Angeles bureau, is an old hand at covering plane crashes. There was the 1986 Aeromexico crash at Cerritos; a DC-9 collided with a small private plane and tumbled into a residential neighborhood, killing 15 people on the ground and 64 on board the two planes. Word of the crash reached the AP at a bureau picnic not far from the crash site, and staffers rushed to the scene.

"When you get there before emergency response is fully in place, they're dealing with the actual fire; they haven't set up roadblocks and stuff like that," Antczak says. "That taught me that you need to get there immediately, to get inside the perimeter, to get to the real people. You don't want people who have been processed through interviews with various authorities and whatnot. You need, basically, to get access. Immediate response is critical. You can't sit around and kind of discuss what's going to happen. You can figure that out while somebody's driving down the road and divide up assignments by phone."

Then there was the 1987 crash of a Pacific Southwest Airlines flight from Los Angeles to San Francisco; a disgruntled airline employee shot the crew, sending the plane into a 23,000-foot plunge. Working the phones in the bureau, "We very quickly got from the FAA the report of gunfire in the cockpit," Antczak recalls.

"Normally, when you think of these big disasters, you think it's going to take a while to sort through the wreckage to find out the cause. But that crash taught me that it's possible to get very close to the actual thing very rapidly, that there is a lot of communication between the air and the ground over stuff that you're unaware of as a passenger."

These lessons in hand, Antczak started assigning staffers to make the calls. Others—reporter Michelle DeArmond, bureau chief Sue Cross, and assistant bureau chief George Garties, among them—were calling emergency agencies. Rogers got the FAA confirmation; the first lead moved

at 5:02. An open line was established between the FAA and the media, and Lota would remain at her desk through the evening, listening for bulletins on her speakerphone.

He sent two staffers to Los Angeles International—one for each level, to cover anyone who might arrive or leave. It wasn't until 5:10, when the second lead was filed, that it was learned that the flight was not bound for Los Angeles at all—it was on its way to San Francisco and then Seattle. At the same time, an LA airport spokesman provided the first glimmer of a cause. The plane had reported mechanical difficulties shortly before the crash and had asked to land at Los Angeles.

Now the AP bureaus in San Francisco and Seattle had to be brought in to send reporters to the airports; the families of passengers on board the plane would no doubt converge there. Meanwhile, staffers had to start working on the mechanical side of the story. What kind of plane had crashed? What was its safety record? What might have gone wrong?

"You're doing several things at once," Antczak says. He was

writing the story, transmitting it, handing out assignments. "A lot of it comes down to, Who's on the phone at the moment? There's a question that has come up; who can I put on the phone?"

At first it was believed that the crash was in Santa Monica Bay. But soon it became clear that it was farther north, off Ventura County. Antczak reached Cindy Webb and redirected her to the airport, along with science writer Matt Fordahl. Antczak told Ken Peters to drive up the coast road: "It's one of those things where you never know what you're going to see. The coast road is literally on the water."

Reporter Jeff Wilson lived right there, in Oxnard; administrative editor Steve Loeper called him at home. His name would go on the story.

This later lead moved at 5:44 p.m.:

AM-CA—Airliner Crash, 4th Ld, 32

OXNARD, Calif. (AP)—An Alaska Airlines Boeing 737 with 70 people aboard crashed in the Pacific Ocean northwest of Los Angeles on Monday after reporting mechanical problems.
MORE

AM-CA—Airliner Crash, 4th Ld, 1st Add, 127

A Coast Guard helicopter, a Navy P-3 airplane and small boats scoured a large debris field rolling in swells off Point Mugu as darkness began to descend on the ocean. There were no immediate signs of survivors.

Flight 261 from Puerto Vallarta, Mexico, to San Francisco and Seattle was reported down 20 miles northwest of Los Angeles International Airport about 3:45 p.m., said Mitch Barker, the Federal Aviation Administration regional spokesman in Seattle.

"Right now they are searching for survivors," said Coast Guard Lt. Jeanne Reincke. "They see a large debris field, but that's all we've heard from them."

FAA operations officer Cynthia Emery said there were 65 crew passengers and five crew members aboard the aircraft.
MORE

AM-CA—Airliner Crash, 4th Ld, 2nd Add, 146

The aircraft was bound for San Francisco International Airport, said airport spokesman Ron Wilson.

Wilson said the aircraft crew reported mechanical difficulties and asked to land at Los Angeles.

"Radar indicates it fell from 17,000 feet and then was lost from radar," Wilson told KRON-TV in San Francisco.

Coroner's officials began arriving at the Oxnard Coast Guard station about 5:30 p.m.

Puerto Vallarta is a resort on Mexico's Pacific coast.

Alaska Airlines is a popular carrier on routes along the West Coast and to Mexican and Canadian destinations.

The airline has more than 80 aircraft, including various models of the Boeing 737 as well as MD-80s.

At the end of 1998, the average age of Alaska's fleet was 7.6 years, the youngest fleet in the nation, according to the airline.

Alaska carried 13.1 million passengers in 1998.

Wilson had just gotten home after a day that began when he arrived at the office at 5:30 a.m.; he had a murderous migraine and had collapsed on the couch when the phone rang. Headache in tow, he jumped into his car and sped over to the Coast Guard station, fully aware that if the crash was well offshore, "I won't see anything."

The Coast Guard spokesmen were not briefing the media pending the arrival of an admiral from Long Beach; all the Harbor Patrol boats had departed for the crash scene. "I've been in the business long enough to know that I had to get out there somehow," says Wilson, who had worked for United Press International and then AP for 26 years.

Wilson went next door to the Coast Guard and Harbor Patrol bases, to Cisco's Landing, a center for sport fishing and whale watching. He asked about hiring a boat. There was only one available, the Ranger 85, and a crew from "Dateline NBC" had locked it up for $1,500.

Wilson talked to the "Dateline" producer. Look, he said. You're looking for footage for your show. To me, this is breaking news. I've got to get this now.

A deal was struck. The AP paid $700 to share the boat with NBC. Wilson and an AP photographer climbed aboard, and they were off. It would take 45 minutes to reach the crash site, a 10-mile ride through "15 to 20-foot seas, hellacious seas. It was terribly cold," Wilson says. The sun had set.

Back at the office, local television stations broadcast video of the crash scene from their helicopters. John Rogers watched and gave Antczak a few paragraphs of description.

"You could immediately see that the impact was devastating," Antczak recalls. "What was floating on the surface was nothing recognizable. It was completely shattered. There wasn't too much to say beyond that. There was never a point where you could say you could see something recognizable as part of a plane. It sort of looked the way the ocean looks after a big storm and all the debris has flown down the channels."

Ken Peters reached the Coast Guard base at Channel Islands harbor; he would pass along quotes and information from officials there. The AP's Washington bureau went to work, collecting information from the FAA and the National Transportation Safety Board.

The number of people on board the plane changed during the night as the airline came up with a better accounting. Finally, it stood at 88. Everyone scrambled

for background on the plane and the airline.

There were lulls in the flow of the story now; they gave Antczak a chance to step back and look at the situation. "You do have to walk around and talk to your reporters individually at some point about what they have. They might not know that they have something that is really useful."

For a time Antczak wrote all the leads. But as the night went on different reporters took turns updating the story, and Antczak reverted to editing the story and filing it on the wire.

There was some confusion about the type of plane that had crashed. At first the FAA said it was a Boeing 737. But Antczak, who had covered aerospace, wondered; when Boeing bought McDonnell Douglas years before, it had occurred to him that it was likely that the 737 someday would be confused with the similar MD-80 series aircraft built by McDonnell Douglas. And in fact, Antczak reached a spokesman for Boeing, who confirmed that the plane was an MD-83.

The Boeing spokesman also provided a history of the aircraft—the number of hours it had spent aloft (25,584), the number of takeoffs and landings it had made (14,345).

At 7:16, Antczak filed a ninth lead. An Alaska Air customer service representative in Los Angeles informed him that the plane had reported problems with its horizontal stabilizer, which maintained the plane's balance. Investigations in the months that followed indicated that the threads of a jackscrew, part of the stabilizer in the tail section, had been stripped. The first indications of the cause of the crash were on the wire less than three hours after Alaska Airlines Flight 261 fell from the sky.

* * *

The crash scene was bathed in the bright lights of boats usually used to catch squid. When the Ranger 85 arrived, the Coast Guard pulled alongside. We need your help, they said. We need the help of every boat out here to collect the wreckage, human and mechanical.

Wilson's headache had not abated. It was cold, and the pungent smell of jet fuel filled the air. His eyes stung. The boat's crew put down nets and brought in bits and pieces of Flight 261.

There were seat cushions. Bits of metal, no bigger than a hubcap. There was tourist stuff: sombreros, maracas, "cheesy souvenirs you would expect people to buy in Mexico."

And there was worse.

"All of a sudden you'd see a shoe or a piece of luggage. We actually captured a shoe with a net, and there was a foot in it. . . . A torso was the largest human part we picked up."

The television crew, Wilson says, was too repulsed to go to the back of the boat and watch what came up in the nets. Wilson stayed. His peculiar training explains a lot—before he was a reporter, he spent four years as a coroner's assistant in Los Angeles, picking up as many as 13 corpses in a night, the victims of car wrecks and fires among them. "It wasn't pleasant, but you kind of get used to it."

His explanation of what he did on the boat? "You're caught up in the moment. You talk yourself into stepping back, to get the big picture. . . . You just sort of move on and get your story."

The boat turned back to port,

and Wilson's phone started working when he was within eight miles of shore. He dictated what he had seen. Some of it was too graphic for the wire. "When you say that someone was blown up, or something like that, that's enough to say, because the descriptions would simply be too horrifying for a reader to encounter," Antczak insists.

The 15th and final lead for morning newspapers moved at 3:17 a.m.:

AM-CA—Airliner Crash, 15th Ld-Writethru, 1145
Airliner with 88 aboard crashes in ocean northwest of Los Angeles
With AP Photos; AP Graphics

By JEFF WILSON
Associated Press Writer

OXNARD, Calif. (AP)—An Alaska Airlines MD-83 bound from Mexico to San Francisco with 88 people aboard crashed in the Pacific Ocean northwest of Los Angeles on Monday after reporting control problems. Only bodies were immediately found.

A large field of debris rolled in big swells off Point Mugu as aircraft and small boats converged on the area just before sunset. Hours later, the powerful lights of squid boats illuminated the inky blackness as cutters and a Navy ship continued the search.

Several bodies were found, said Coast Guard Lt. Chuck Diorio.

On the water, deckhands on a fishing boat collected body parts, Mexican toys, a stuffed animal, a shoe, cushions and aircraft insulation. "It's pretty disturbing, but somebody's got to do it," deckhand David Searles, 31, told reporters aboard the boat.

A utility vessel with debris on deck arrived in nearby Port Hueneme after dark.

Flight 261 from Puerto Vallarta, Mexico, to San Francisco and Seattle was reported down at 4:36 p.m., said airline spokesman Jack Evans.

There were 83 passengers and five crewmembers aboard, Evans said. Of the passengers, 32 were bound for San Francisco, 47 were bound for Seattle, three were continuing on to Eugene, Ore., and one to Fairbanks, Alaska. The two pilots were based in Los Angeles and the three flight attendants were based in Seattle.

The passengers included three Alaska Airlines employees, four employees of sister airline Horizon and 23 family or friends of those seven employees or the crew.

"We will do anything and everything to find out exactly what transpired," Alaska Chairman John Kelly told a late-night press conference in Los Angeles, holding out hope that there would be survivors.

"I am an eternal optimist," Kelly said. "That's some cold water, some deep water. It's not the best thing you'd ever want in the world, but miracles have happened before."

Kelly said the pilot had more than 10,000 hours of flying time with Alaska and the first officer had more then 8,000 hours.

The crash site was 40 miles northwest of Los Angeles International Airport, about 10 miles offshore between the mainland port of Oxnard and Anacapa Island.

In San Francisco, four people waiting for the flight were led away by airline workers. A few relatives came to Los Angeles International, where they tended to by psychologists and clergy, said American Red Cross spokeswoman Brenda-Victoria Castillo.

"Every resource is out there to find people," said Coast Guard Capt. George Wright. "We're actively searching for survivors.... In 58-degree water temperature, people can survive. We're not going to quit until we're positive there's absolutely no chance."

The plane reported mechanical problems and requested a diversion to Los Angeles, FAA operations officer Diana Joubert said. The diversion was granted and the plane was headed to Los Angeles when it crashed, Joubert said.

"Radar indicates if fell from 17,000 feet and then was lost from radar," San Francisco airport spokesman Ron Wilson told KRON-TV in San Francisco.

A National Park Service ranger on Anacapa Island saw the airliner go down and was first to report it, said spokeswoman Susan Smith at the Channel Islands National Park headquarters in Ventura Harbor.

"He observed a jet going down in the Santa Barbara Channel. From his observation it was nose first," Smith said.

The weather was clear at the crash site, and the water typically has a temperature in the low 50s this time of year. Water depth estimates at the site range from 300 feet to 750 feet.

Evans said the pilot had reported having problems with the "stabilizer trim" shortly before the plane crashed.

If the pilots were having trouble trimming the horizontal stabilizer, it would mean that they were having difficulty bringing the plane into the proper pitch up or down.

The stabilizer is brought into balance, or "trimmed," by spinning a wheel in the cockpit. When a plane has the proper trim, its nose will fly level, instead of pitching up or down.

Evans said the aircraft had no previous stabilizer trim problems. He also said the plane had a low-level service check on Jan. 11 and a more thorough check as part of normal maintenance last January.

The MD-83 is part of the MD-80 series of aircraft built by McDonnell Douglas' commercial aircraft unit, which is now part of Boeing.

John Thom, Boeing's Douglas aircraft unit spokesman, said the plane was a model MD-83 that was delivered to Alaska Airlines in May 1992.

The plane had logged 25,584 flight hours and 14,315 "cycles," Evans said. A "cycle" includes one takeoff and one landing.

Evans said the plane last was serviced Sunday, although he could not describe the nature of the servicing. He said the plane got what is known as an "A" check on Jan. 11 and a "C" check on Jan. 13, 1999. He said a "C" check is most comprehensive, an "A" check the least comprehensive.

Alaska Airlines is a popular carrier on routes along the West Coast and to Mexican and Canadian destinations.

The airline has more than 80 aircraft, including MD-80s and Boeing 737s.

At the end of 1998, the average age of Alaska's fleet was 7.6 years, the youngest fleet in the nation, according to the airline.

Alaska carried 13.1 million passengers in 1998.

Alaska Airlines, which has a distinctive image of an Eskimo painted on the tails of its planes, has an excellent safety record. It serves more than 40 cities in Alaska, Canada, Mexico and five Western states.

The most recent fatal crash in the United States involving an MD-80 series jet was last summer's American Airlines accident in Little Rock, Ark. Eleven people were killed and 110 injured when an MD-82 landed in high wind and heavy rain, ran off the runway, broke apart and caught fire.

The MD-80 is a twin-jet version of the more widely known DC-9, with a single aisle and an engine on each side of the tail. It went into service in 1980 and has had at least five variations that offer different ranges and seating capacities.

Alaska Airlines, based in Seattle, operates several flights from Puerto Vallarta, a resort on Mexico's Pacific coast, to San Jose, San Francisco and other California cities.

The airline had two fatal accidents in the 1970s, both in Alaska, according to Airsafe.com, a Web site that tracks plane crashes.

In 1971, an Alaska Airlines Boeing 727-100 approaching Juneau crashed into a mountain slope after the crew had received misleading navigational information. All 104 passengers and seven crew members and [sic] were killed.

In 1976, one passenger was killed when a 727 overran the runway after landing in Ketchikan.

On the way in, Wilson also called AP Network News and was interviewed about what he had seen. When he arrived, after midnight, he gave an impromptu news conference for television and radio. He returned to his home and then went back to work on the story at 5 a.m. In the days to come he would comb the beaches, looking for wreckage that might wash up, and interview the families of crash victims.

The 15th lead was the last one of that cycle, but it was far from the end of the story. It was written again and updated repeatedly for afternoon newspapers, and then for the next day, and the next day. Managing a story like this one means more than pumping the leads out one after another.

"Particularly in a 24-hour newsroom, you have to hold some people back to be fresh for a later time; you have to assign some people to report for the future rather than the current cycle, you have to get in food for the bureau staff and find accommodations for the field people," says Garties, the assistant bureau chief.

Fordahl, the science writer, eventually became the main reporter on the technical aspects of the investigation. He used numerous Web sites, among other tools, to track the plane's history. Reporter Tom Verdin wrote an early sidebar on liability issues in ocean crashes. Reporter Leon Drouin Keith took on the job of writing thumbnail sketches of the victims, trying to put a face on these people who died en masse and in horror.

Wilson came to grips with their loss a year later, when he was the pool reporter covering a memorial for the 88 who died. The survivors had set up a 40-foot wall, covered with pictures of smiling people who all died together on Jan. 31, 2000. In front of the wall they had placed some of the victims' possessions: a kayak, an uncompleted afghan, knitting needles in place. Pudding cups. A deck of cards.

"That really sent a shiver up your spine. You realize that you distance yourself from it all or you can't do what you do. Same thing as the coroner's office," Wilson says.

"It was unbelievable. It was very emotional. . . . I got a lumpy throat, too."

2 What Is News?

When a plane crashes in the water off Los Angeles, there's no question: It's news. But what if an animal control officer in Biloxi, Miss., is killed by a train as he chases a pit bull down the tracks?

Yes, said Ron Harrist. And so, on a Wednesday morning in March, newspapers across Mississippi got a brief story about the death of Nathan Mitchell, 33, who was struck near the Camelia Street crossing after receiving a call from a woman who said that a pit bull was loose and was threatening her child.

Harrist is the AP's news editor in Jackson, Miss. He arrives at work at 7:15 a.m. each day and sets about deciding what's news and what's not.

He looks at the stories offered by the state's newspapers and considers whether readers outside the immediate community would be interested.

The dogcatcher's death? "That's obviously a box in a paper somewhere," he says. A story about federal funds that would go to improve air and water quality along the Gulf Coast? "If I was across the state, in Picayune, I would want to know about it."

In the course of this day he will deploy his staff of six to cover a state of 2.8 million people. There will be some breaking stories: The Jackson police chief, embroiled in a scandal, will announce that he is stepping down. The Delta Democrat Times in Greenville will be sold. Legislative leaders will agree to open some committee meetings to the public.

His sports writer, Ralph Russo, will contribute a story on the prospects of Mississippi schools in the NCAA basketball tournament. Staffer Timothy Brown will write a story analyzing a spate of layoffs in the state in recent weeks. One Mississippi story will find its way onto the national wire—a piece about the rumored purchase of Worldcom, the nation's second-largest long-distance provider, based in Jackson.

It's all news, along with the story about Jackson County authorities urging motorists to slow down after two crossing guards were struck and another about a minister's son being charged with setting fire to his father's church. Harrist is the one who decides what gets on the wire. It's a little like being an air traffic controller, he says. At every moment, he's picking up stories or casting them aside, based on the time and the number of people he has at his disposal.

"To me, time is everything," he says. "You have to have a little clock in your head, and you have to say, 'We have this to do, we have this to do.' You have to have that little clock saying, 'All right, I know that by 9 a.m. I've lost 90 percent of my evening papers.' "

But he also uses his sense of what's news. And that has changed over the years.

"I remember when I first started in this, certain things like fatalities were big news in this state. People wanted to know who died, particularly in accidents. And as the state grew and different things changed, it became less important," Harrist says. A car crash is no longer statewide news.

Louis D. Boccardi, the AP's president and chief executive officer, has seen the same changes nearly everywhere. Until the mid-1970s the AP operated a "local bureau" in New York City, with correspondents in the city's neighborhoods, in the courts, at police headquarters. They covered the city wall to wall; no development was too small. "And one day, we looked around and there was no more need, no more call, no more place for this kind of day-to-day, 'it happened in Bronx County Court today, so here it is.' So AP local disappeared," Boccardi says.

The same kind of reporting was once the norm nationally and internationally as well. The AP would report something merely because it was said in the German Bundestag or the Japanese Diet or the U.S. Senate. Today that would be considered minutiae; anyone who wants a verbatim account of what happens in the U.S. Congress probably will watch it on C-SPAN. The "level of reporting" is no longer the same, Boccardi says.

Some of these changes have to do with the torrent of information in an information age. "The flood of it is just extraordinary, on a scale that was unimaginable even just a few years ago," Boccardi says.

So it has become reporters' responsibility to provide "explanation and understanding and background." Not long ago, "there was even a kind of bias against this kind of thing. The old way was just straight 'he said-she said,' and that's what the AP was supposed to do," Boccardi says. "We have moved off that. . . . What the times demand is helping

the reader cope with this flow of information which is beyond anybody's capacity to deal with."

Other changes: "The language you'll see and the subjects you'll see covered in the daily newspaper now. I don't consider myself ancient, but in my time at a newspaper, one of my jobs was to watch for certain words that you just couldn't put in the paper. The body-part words and some others. And now they slide through, seemingly perfectly naturally. And there are subjects, a frankness to some of the subjects covered, that's certainly new.

"The reporting of personal kinds of information about public figures, entertainment personalities and others, is certainly more widespread than it used to be.

"The question of anonymity is a much larger question than it was 20 or more years ago, partly because of the Watergate influence on the reporting field, maybe in part because governments are a little more difficult to deal with. There is more official secrecy, more hurdles. . . . You can't get it officially, so you have to get it on a source basis."

Speed still matters, just as it did in the days when AP reporters raced their competitors at United Press to the phone to dictate their stories. "If it's breaking, we want to be first," Ron Harrist says. If anything, the pressure is greater than ever; news reaches the public almost instantaneously, via all-news television networks and the Internet, and everyone else has to keep pace.

But some things haven't changed. News is still "anything that will make anybody say 'my, my,' " says Boccardi—though it might take a more extraordinary story to get a rise out of readers, and their note of exclamation might be a bit more colorful than that.

News is still fair and objective—though today's reporters must walk the fine line between putting events in perspective and giving their own opinions. The AP was among the most influential forces in bringing objectivity to American journalism. As a cooperative, owned by all sorts of newspapers, it could not offer a partisan slant, and this eventually became the standard for all.

"My business is to communicate facts," wrote the AP's first Washington correspondent, Lawrence Gobright, in 1862. "My instructions do not allow me to make any comment upon the facts. My dispatches are sent to papers of all manners of politics. I therefore confine myself to what I consider legitimate news and try to be truthful and impartial."

And news, above all, is accurate. "Without accuracy, you've got no story at all," says Allen Breed, the AP's Southeast regional reporter. "In fact, you've done a disservice."

This is not to say that the AP has never been inaccurate. There are mistakes made every day, and some have become legend—most spectacularly, the story of how the AP botched the verdict in the Lindbergh kidnapping, a moment so traumatic that it was the stuff of AP nightmares for decades.

The abduction of the 19-month-old son of Charles Lindbergh—the first man to fly across the Atlantic, the greatest hero of his age—was one of the biggest stories of the century. The AP's Frank Jamieson won a Pulitzer Prize for his coverage of the 11-week-long search for the child, which ended with the discovery of the toddler's body five miles from the Lindberghs' New Jersey home.

Bruno Hauptmann, a Bronx carpenter, was charged with the crime. His trial in Flemington, N.J., began in January 1935; the public's obsession with the case was unrelenting, and the AP's New Jersey bureau chief was determined to get out the first word on the verdict. This was his plan: An AP staffer would smuggle a small telegraph transmitter into the courtroom, under his coat. When the verdict was handed down, he would send a message to another staffer who was hiding in the attic, who in turn would put the news directly on the wire.

The jury began deliberations at 11:15 a.m. on Feb. 13. Eleven hours later it reported that it had reached a verdict. The AP's man with a transmitter was in the courtroom, along with other AP reporters who would report the story more traditionally.

What happened next has never been fully explained. The man in the attic cut into the national wire with a flash: "FLEMINGTON—VERDICT REACHED GUILTY AND LIFE." He would later say that he had clearly heard the code for a guilty verdict with a life sentence—four signals—though the staffer with the transmitter denied sending it and in fact no verdict had yet been handed down.

For 11 minutes, the AP was on the wire with the wrong verdict in a case that many would call the trial of the century. The jury did convict Hauptmann, but it sentenced him to death.

"This error seemed almost a personal tragedy" to the staff of the AP, Oliver Gramling would write in his history, "AP: The Story of News." It is true that the AP had made big mistakes before (in the election of 1884 it had reported that James G. Blaine won New York, which would have made him president; he hadn't, and he wasn't). But for a news service that took pride in putting accuracy before speed, it was a humbling moment. The AP's mistake was news in itself.

Sixty-five years later, on Election Night, 2000, the AP made news of a very different sort. The closest election in more than a century was ending in a photo finish; Voter News Service, a partnership of the television networks and the AP that conducts exit polls and provides vote totals, was projecting that George W. Bush had won Florida and the election.

One after another the networks fell into line.

Only the AP held back. Dozens of editors at member newspapers called the AP in Miami, Washington, New York. Some were irate; deadlines loomed. When was the AP going to call this election?

But the AP had its own vote counters, and their numbers told a different story. Sandy Johnson, the AP's Washington bureau chief, consulted her analysts. No, they agreed. This is just too close. At 3:11 a.m. the AP put out an advisory: Though the networks had called the race for Bush, outstanding votes "could allow a change of the lead." And that is how it stayed for five weeks, until the AP reported that Gore had decided to concede, 35 days after his campaign's obituary had been printed prematurely.

"The AP has had many 'finest hours' over the years," wrote James Daubel, publisher of The News-Messenger of Fremont, Ohio, but the election "ranks right up there with the best of them."

Because if it isn't accurate, it isn't news. It's fiction.

3 Ideas and How to Get Them

Main Street Welcomes McDonald's—but Worries

By TED ANTHONY
AP National Writer

COUDERSPORT, Pa. (AP)—The day it opened, it seemed all Potter County streamed in. Children jostled for Happy Meals. The judge visited the drive-thru (Quarter Pounder, apple pie and Diet Coke, scuttlebutt had it). Downtown merchants sent flowers.

"Now," said 15-year-old Matt Seeley, "we don't have to drive 40 miles for a Big Mac anymore."

On that day last September, two American institutions—one the stuff of tradition, the other the stuff of all-beef patties and sesame-seed buns—converged. On that day, McDonald's met Main Street.

There are fewer and fewer towns in the land where "Would you like fries with that?" is not a familiar refrain. Until McDonald's No. 20,160 arrived with its 57 seats, three outdoor tables and golden-arch architecture scaled down to minimum obtrusiveness, this

Allegheny River Valley town of 3,200 souls was one of them.

Coudersport is the sort of unblemished town that late-20th-century Americans dream about—full of mom-and-pop businesses, public spaces and first-name greetings. Until last year, there were two diners, an old-time hotel-restaurant, a couple of pizza places and three family restaurants, but no national fast-food chains for miles around.

Many citizens were ready for the McDonald's that opened on the edge of their downtown. It meant a spot on the map. It meant that they were plugged into the modern American goulash of advertising, commerce and popular culture.

It also meant apprehension—about what might come next.

* * *

"Some of the merchants here are deathly afraid of this McDonald's," Jeff

Kazimer was saying last summer, a few months before the Golden Arches arrived.

Kazimer (one of Coudersport's two barbers) and five companions were eating lunch in the Crittenden Hotel, considered the borough's classiest restaurant. But conversation veered to the town's new eatery.

"Teen-agers—all they do is walk the streets here. This'll give them some self-esteem," said Shirlee Leete, a writer and state police photographer. "This will give jobs to a lot of people who haven't been hired in a lot of places."

"It's a sign that we're making progress," said Mavis Macklem, who runs Coudersport Insurance.

Even Walter Baker, the president of Coudersport's Chamber of Commerce and owner of the Crittenden, concurred. "It'll bring more people into town," he said. "That can only be good."

When McDonald's came calling, concerns surfaced: Would gaudy signs and car-culture architecture push Coudersport toward garishness? Would traffic be unbearable? Would kids loiter and make trouble, straining the borough's four police officers?

More ominously, would Burger King, Pizza Hut, even Wal-Mart follow, taking business from downtown? Would Coudersport lose its uniqueness?

"When the first franchise comes to town, it's generally a wake-up call for the community. People begin to ask: 'What do we want?'" says Kennedy Smith, director of the National Main Street Center, part of the National Trust for Historic Preservation.

"This is exactly the time to look at it," she says. "In 10 years, when there's the Pizza Hut and the strip mall out there, it's simply too late."

* * *

Pennsylvania has the nation's largest rural population; in 1990, 31.1 percent of its 11.8 million people lived in rural areas, according to the U.S. Census. Research by the Center for Rural Pennsylvania tells a familiar story—small-town retailers fleeing to the strip malls, older downtowns struggling, new development in outlying areas.

Many Main Streets have withered or tapered off into netherworlds of chain motels, chain restaurants, chain muffler shops, chain minimarts.

"You can airdrop yourself into some places in the United States and not know where you are," says Carol Truppi, director of programs for Scenic America, a preservation group.

That may not be desirable, but it is understandable. An estimated 95 percent of Americans have eaten at McDonald's, and marketers work so hard to make standardized fast food an integral part of the adscape that consumer-citizens start seeing a gap when it isn't there.

"Consumerism is the future. It's how we're going to be tied to each other," says Bill Caldwell, just retired as Potter County's jobs officer.

But the sentiment doesn't come easy. Self-reliance—especially the culinary variety—is ingrained in this region.

Coudersport, carved from a pine-hemlock forest 192 years ago, has always been defined by the outdoors. Hunting—deer, turkey, grouse, bear—is front-page news. Local histories brim with tales of dinner killed in the woods or pulled from the streams.

Even today, 40 percent of the county's homes are hunting cabins, and McDonald's sits a few yards from the place where Nelson Goodsell caught the county's largest speckled trout in June 1876.

Those very hunters, though, helped entice McDonald's. On weekends, they come from all Pennsylvania's corners to camp, hunt, fish, go snowmobiling. Lately, they want modern amenities: Hot tubs are supplanting fireplaces; elaborate TV-stereo systems are being installed.

And in the morning, they line up at McDonald's.

Downtown Coudersport, meanwhile, remains strong, and not because of the kitschy gift shops that have reinvigorated so many historic small communities. This Main Street is real; residents use it for daily business. Thus far, aside from a small J.C. Penney, a Sears that closed years ago, several gas stations and a Sheetz convenience store that opened in 1989, virtually all business activity has been independent.

Coudersport once faced the same fate as many of its neighbors: population drift, fading industry, a youth exodus.

But in the mid-1980s, entrepreneur John Regis' company, Adelphia Cable Communications, began growing rapidly. He kept its headquarters in Coudersport; Adelphia's increasing success brought a growing base of skilled labor—today, about 500 jobs—to the region.

Potter County has a vigorous economy. Add that to increased traffic along scenic U.S. 6, and McDonald's—with nearly 60 jobs, culled from 150 applications—seems a natural addition, another indication of Coudersport's survival.

"McDonald's knows where to locate," Truppi says. "If they locate there, it's probably going to work. And that's a good indicator for this small town."

* * *

Since 1978, Gene Walsh, whose GIW Enterprises is the McDonald's franchisee in this chunk of Pennsylvania, has dedicated his career to making a national corporation work on a local level. To Walsh, McDonald's is a family business.

His son, Bob, runs the McDonald's in Towanda, 70 miles east; his daughter, Debbie, runs the one in Mansfield, 30 miles away. GIW also operates the McDonald's in Wellsboro, another nearby Route 6 town.

"It's just an amazing company," says Walsh, a former driver for UPS. "There's always somebody who wants to bad-mouth it, but it's like a family."

McDonald's has long encouraged this approach. Eighty-five percent of its U.S. stores are franchises, granted to businesspeople who in many cases live in the communities where they operate.

"Some people saw us as displacing the local mom and pop," says Chuck Ebeling, a spokesman for McDonald's Corp. "I think the transformation in 40 years is that we are mom and pop now. We're not an unknown entity coming to town."

Walsh, too, while realizing that the Route 6 location is crucial—"We can't be on a back road and attract just locals," he says—wants most business to come from the community, not drivers-through.

And he makes a point of buying everything he can locally, from hardware to topsoil. Still, corporate structure limits him. Potter County is famous for potatoes—a once-giant farm, Potato City USA, is six miles east—but none of McDonald's fries are made from local crops. Everything comes off a McDonald's supply truck.

Historically, fast food has inhabited highway strips, interstate exit ramps and edge cities. Now it is expanding into untapped locales: historic areas, campuses, airports, hospitals—and small-town business districts like Coudersport's.

"They have to just keep pushing out and getting into these places. It's where the bodies are," says Mike Kennedy, an American Express analyst. "They'll downsize and create on a smaller scale to get new bodies to buy their hamburgers and not somebody else's."

* * *

Perhaps surprisingly, the very things Americans so treasure about Main Street—Victorian and Greek Revival architecture that evokes grand democracy—are themselves the 19th-century version of standardization.

"Years ago, these facades they love so much were being cranked out, too," says Richard Francaviglia, who spent two decades studying small-town business districts for his book, "Main Street Revisited."

"Main Street itself embodies standardization and the whole concept of assimilation into a nationally held system of beliefs and values."

Today, those values often include the corporate brand names that are just now making their way to Coudersport. Besides McDonald's, says Borough Manager Marlin Moore, Burger King has expressed interest, Pizza Hut has poked around and the Super 8 motel chain has looked at property on the edge of town.

And then there's Wal-Mart. Moore says the discount heavyweight once took an option on property near here but never built a store; Jack Halloran says he'd simply close Halloran Hardware if a Wal-Mart opened.

"This is a town of generations, of businesses passed on," says Linda Russell, who works at Hauber's Jewelers on Main Street. "And all of a sudden, up shows McDonald's and Sheetz, and it's a very visual reminder that those days you so loved aren't there anymore."

So the people of Coudersport are wary, and perhaps rightly so.

"There is no place in America today that will remain special by accident," says Edward McMahon, director of the American Greenways Program at the Conservation Fund, a nonprofit organization.

"Without exception, the places that are considered outstanding have taken charge of their destiny," he says. "If Coudersport does nothing, in 10 years there will be seven fast-food restaurants and the whole place will go down the tubes. They have to say: 'We want to stand out.'"

* * *

On a cold February morning, months after McDonald's arrival, Jack Halloran arrives at his hardware store with a steaming cup of coffee. Underneath the Crittenden, Jeff Kazimer is bibbing up the day's first trim.

At Mickey's Diner, Shirlee Leete takes a seat and lights the first in a succession of Misty Menthols. Behind her, the police chief sips coffee. An acquaintance returns a dime borrowed for parking.

The tables are full, and Leete knows each occupant. The omelets, jammed with fresh stuff, spill over plates and are never the same shape. "Curb your tongue," warns a sign, "or you might be tonguing the curb."

Finally, there is 78-year-old Mickey Goodwin herself, who for three decades has risen at 4 a.m., made doughnuts and taken no guff—and who has never set foot in McDonald's.

"Regulars are very loyal," says her daughter, Nancy Giannone. "McDonald's is affecting everyone a little bit, but they'll always come in for Mom's fry cakes and glazed Danish."

Meanwhile, at McDonald's, people queue up for Egg McMuffins, where the eggs fit the McMuffins perfectly and there is no ordering "the usual."

"At McDonald's," laments Halloran, "the cook doesn't come out and talk to you."

McDonald's will always be clean, quick, and—with a few regional variations—the same. Main Street may not be so unchanging; the arrival of the fast-food behemoth could signal the start of a civic deathwatch.

Then again, maybe not.

"You see a lot of towns die. Somehow, Coudersport hangs on," says Caldwell, the retired jobs officer. "Diversity has been the lifeblood of the town. If something fell through, there was something else to fall back on. And I think this is an evolution—something a little more diverse that might help us hang on a little bit longer."

He's a bit embarrassed by it—not much, just a little, because he is not the kind of man who is easily embarrassed—but when Ted Anthony has a story idea, he sometimes whispers it into a digital recorder.

It "may seem kind of stupid, when you look at it. There's an old movie, 'Night Shift,' where Michael Keaton has a handheld cassette and he says things into it like, 'Idea: Feed the tuna mayonaise while it's still alive.' I think a lot of reporters would be put off by that, because it seems geeky.

"But the fact is that some of our best ideas come directly from the world around us rather than from sitting behind our desks thinking about story ideas. In our encounters with the world around us, we see hundreds of things, in every walk we take to the car, the subway, in every drive we take to the mall, and most of those things just pass through our minds and go out the other end. I think that the question of dealing with story ideas is more a question of harnessing story ideas than finding ideas. We all have these ideas, but we don't necessarily recognize them as ideas. We say, 'That's weird,' or 'That's interesting—I

wonder what makes that tick.' But then it just passes out of our minds."

Record those ideas on a digital recorder or in a notebook, and nine out of 10 of them will become nothing. But the 10th idea, he says, might be a great story.

"I've gotten ideas from grocery store bulletin boards. I've gotten ideas from classified ads. I've gotten ideas from things I've passed along the road and just wondered what they were."

Reporters, he says, often "put down their antennas. We're conditioned to look for story ideas when we're at municipal meetings, when we're covering something, when we're working. . . . It's not so much a question of thinking about ideas all the time; it's simply a matter of recognizing the ideas when they come. Because most of us are journalists because we have those ideas. We don't have those ideas because we're journalists. The trick is to make sure that all facets of our lives are funneling into that idea mill."

While visiting Keene, N.H., to work on a story, Anthony went out to eat at a Thai restaurant. In the course of the meal it occurred to him that he was listening to a Muzak version of "The House of the Rising Sun." And he got to thinking about the path this old song took, from folk ballad to something one might hear while eating pad thai in a New England town. In the months that followed he tracked the song back to the moment it entered the larger world, in 1937, when a Kentucky girl sang it into the recorder of a folklorist from the Library of Congress. He listened to scores of versions: reggae, jazz, heavy metal—a mind-numbing potpourri of "Rising Sun" covers. He talked with singers and musicologists. And he came away with a story about how culture spreads in our times.

"I try to write stories that take the everyday and explore what it means," he says. "Often, when I'm writing stories, people will say, 'That's not a story,' or 'You're making too much of that. Everything doesn't have a deeper meaning.' But many things do."

Some of his best ideas, he says, are "things that are kernels of ideas in stories that are about something else." Once he was reading a little story about the small town of Crabtree, Pa., and its plans to do some road maintenance. In the last paragraph the story said the townspeople would be "looking to their three congressmen in order to make this reality."

"I'm thinking to myself, 'This is a tiny town. Three congressmen?' So I make a phone call. I find out that Crabtree is at the corner of three congressional districts and that this borough of about 1,500 people is represented by three people in Washington. So I went there and did a story about it."

The McDonald's story had similar origins. Visiting an old girlfriend in Elmira, N.Y., Anthony picked up the local paper, the Star-Gazette. Deep inside the Pennsylvania section he found an eight-inch story about how the nation's largest fast-food chain was coming to Coudersport in six months. Years before, as a reporter for The Patriot-News of Harrisburg, Pa., he had traveled around the state; Coudersport was among his favorite towns, with a charming Main Street and a picture-perfect courthouse. "On a snowy winter's day, it can double for Bedford Falls in 'It's a Wonderful Life,' " he says.

Anthony is interested in the changes in the American landscape and how everyday things that are often taken for granted shape our lives in large ways. An example is fast-food chains, which have "changed the way we eat, shaped the way we view businesses and franchises and chains—and, possibly most importantly, helped to alter the way our communities operate," he says.

Maybe, he thought, there's something to learn in Coudersport.

He called Shirlee Leete, the Star-Gazette's stringer in Coudersport. She told Anthony that if he came to town, she would gather a few local businesspeople to chat with him. So on a summer day Anthony sat down to lunch at the Crittenden Hotel with Leete; Jeff Kazimer, the town barber, who operated out of a basement shop just below the Crittenden; Mavis Macklem, who ran Coudersport Insurance; Jack Halloran, the proprietor of Halloran Hardware up the street; and Walter Baker, the president of the borough's Chamber of Commerce and, it turned out, the owner of and chef at the Crittenden.

It was a freewheeling discussion. People were wondering

about the aesthetics of having McDonald's in the community, about traffic and loitering and the possibility that other chains, even a Wal-Mart, would follow in McDonald's wake. For Anthony this was an ideal starting point. Their concerns were specific to this little town, but they applied all across America as well.

"There are two ingredients that make a story exceptional," he says. "If you can write a story about something totally, utterly unique, you probably can hook people. And if you write a story about something that's universal and appeals to an interest in everyone, you can probably hook people as well. But the real trick is to combine them: to write a story about a unique place in time, a completely unique situation, but also make sure it taps into universal themes."

And so he began his reporting, getting to know Coudersport more intimately. Early on, when his editors approved his story proposal, AP's television arm was interested in doing the story. We'll send a camera crew along with you, they said.

No way, said Anthony. When you're reporting in a rural town

and trying to get people to trust you, you can't go in with cameras rolling.

"The way to do it is to go back and go back again, get your hair cut at the barber, which I did. Hang out in the hardware store, eat at the diner, and talk to those people while you're participating in their lives, not just coming in and big-footing things," he says.

"I'll tell you one thing I do, and some people think it's silly. When I report in the Midwest, I take out my earring, because I think that it's hard enough in some areas of the Midwest to say you're a reporter from New York and get any response. But to say you're a reporter from New York with an earring is probably the kiss of death. It may seem like a tiny thing; it may seem like an obnoxious thing. But the fact is that can make the difference between good material and bad material."

In New York Anthony dresses with a certain style. He wears eccentric ties. He has been known to come into the office in African-print shirts. This is not what he wears while reporting a story.

"I hate the way I dress when I'm on assignment, but I do it deliberately. Sometimes I'll wear normal stuff, but most of the time I'll wear a plain shirt with no tie, plain pants and plain shoes. I don't want to be nondescript. I want my clothes to be nondescript," he says, so that he can deal with all kinds of people, regardless of their station or attitude.

He began to accumulate the detail that gives his stories their richness. He went through local histories of Coudersport, hoping to learn more about this town's soul and pick up some facts from the past that might be useful in the present. "I found a little factoid about the guy who caught the county's largest speckled trout more than a century ago. They talked about where the catch happened, and it occurred to me that it was very near where the McDonald's was going up."

He writes down everything and anything he sees that might be at all useful.

"You can never have too much detail—which is different from, you can never use too much detail. You have to use self-discipline in the amount of detail you use in a story. You should not be using self-discipline in the amount of detail you gather. Obviously, you can't gather every

detail, but if you notice something, write it down, simply
because the fact that you've
noticed it means that it's significant even if it doesn't consciously
seem significant to you. You
wouldn't have noticed it otherwise. There's hundreds of thousands of things to notice in any
scene, in anything you're doing.
And the fact that you've noticed
one of them means that it's bub-
bled up to the surface, and that in
itself makes it potentially useful."

Besides, he says, you don't
really know whether a detail will
be useful until you write.

Of late, Anthony has brought a
digital camera along on his assignments. He takes pictures and
looks at them when he's writing,
much as a director might make
storyboards before shooting a
film. When he went hiking and
camping on a mountain with a
group of people who were looking for a missing plane, he came
back with pictures that he taped
to a cardboard box that he put
atop his computer screen.

"I was able to say that the
leaves were still on the trees, that
the grass was still green. And
these are very relevant things
when you're searching for a plane

under brush. I also described the
brush and the path and the pine
needles and the sky and everything perfectly."

Coudersport was only one part
of the story. Anthony wanted to
look at the idea of Main Street in
America—to look at whether the
popular, idealized conception of
the virtues of small-town life was
valid. Anthony also wanted to
know more about McDonald's
and about the philosophy of fast
food. He read a book about the
corporation's history, "Behind the
Arches." He interviewed folks at
McDonald's headquarters in Oak
Park, Ill. He spoke to the guy
who was opening the Coudersport McDonald's, Gene Walsh;
only then did he realize that this
was not necessarily a story about
a big outside corporation bulling
its way into a small town; Walsh
was from Mansfield, two towns
over, and he ran his franchises as a
family business.

He also talked with a number
of experts who are quoted in the
story: Edward McMahon, director
of the American Greenways Program at the Conservation Fund;
writer Richard Francaviglia; Mike
Kennedy, an American Express
analyst—and others who are not.

"I learned pretty early on . . . that there were these great people who had these great insights, and they would, from a purely practical standpoint, add another source and credibility and facts to my story," he says. The son of two college professors, he does not distrust academia, as some reporters do. But sometimes he will call experts merely to get background or lead him to other, more appropriate sources or to confirm that he is on the right track.

He has accumulated and continues to accumulate an extraordinary collection of experts and has assembled them in a computerized Rolodex, searchable by keyword, in Microsoft Outlook.

"Every time I come across someone who is interesting, I create an address card for them with a phone number, but what I also do is I put in about eight or nine keywords for each of them that when you search as a free-form text file, it comes up. So if I have, say, 'franchising'—that's a good example from the McDonald's story—then I'll have four or five people who come up who can talk about that. . . .

"What you always have to be doing is be on the lookout for sources. This is the same thing as ideas. You have to approach your Rolodex the same way you address your idea bank. You have to be open to these sources wherever you find them. If you're reading something that quotes someone who may be of interest in the future, you write that down. Even if you don't have a phone number for them, you put them in your Rolodex with a keyword. And then when you need them you know that they exist, you know maybe where they're from, and then you go pursue the phone number. Pretty much every Sunday in The New York Times, I get about six or seven new sources just from reading the Week in Review, from reading the Arts and Leisure section, that type of thing. And I just write down the names and I just throw the stack of notes in my bag, and when I come in on Monday, I put them in the computer Rolodex."

He also uses experts listed on university Web sites, and he uses Profnet, a Web site of the Public Relations Newswire (www.profnet.com). It lists experts available to answer questions on many topics; it also will circulate queries from reporters looking for specialists on other issues. "If I put out a query, I will get back 30 or 40 responses, and I'll use maybe two of them," Anthony says. "And the other 35 go into the Rolodex," to be used for another story.

Four times a year he goes through special issues of Publisher's Weekly devoted to the season's new books, looking for books that are of interest; he writes down the author's name and the name of the book and publisher and puts it in his Rolodex. He buys books that might be useful, even though he knows that it is unlikely he will read them anytime soon, because they might be useful some day. An example: "Behind the Arches," which he bought at a bookstore years before he wrote the Coudersport story.

"My Rolodex is in the computer, my Rolodex is on my bookshelves, my Rolodex is my head, my Rolodex is in all the magazines and newspapers that I read," he says. "It all channels into one big database of not necessarily definite sources but potential sources that are just kind of waiting in the wings for when I might need them."

For this story Anthony visited Coudersport three times: once before McDonald's opened, once on its opening day, and once six months later. (Actually, he visited a fourth time: "I passed through after that to eat a Big Mac. It had nothing to do with the story.") The key moment, he says, was at the grand opening, when a patron told him, "Now we don't have to drive 40 miles for a Big Mac anymore."

"That was it, to me, in a nutshell. Here was this town that everybody loved for its character, yet there was a yearning to be connected—to partake in this corner of mass culture and fast food that everybody else has within reach. There was the tension—yes, we want our community the way it is, but . . . we also want to belong to the bigger picture that everybody else thinks is so cool.

"And from there, my story fell into place. It was a tale of a town that wanted two things—yesterday and today. They wanted to be unique—and to be like everyone else. To have Mickey's Diner AND Mickey D's. And in the end, for Coudersport, there was room for both."

The toughest part of writing, for Anthony, is what's left on the editing room floor. "It's hard, especially when people are enthusiastic about the story, and you interview them and they don't appear."

He quotes two of his bosses. Pete Mattiace, his first bureau chief in Charleston, W.Va., told him, "Whenever you think you're done with a story, you can always cut 10 percent." And his current editor, Bruce DeSilva, is fond of saying, "Take out everything that's good in a story when you're done with it, and all that's left will be great."

"I grow attached to things," he says. "I grow attached to words and phrases and quotes, and it's very hard to get rid of them. And I fight and scream and curse and throw things at my bosses when they want to take it out. But ultimately, it's probably a good idea."

4 Ideas II: Listening to America

Death of a Bully

By JULES LOH
AP Special Correspondent

SKIDMORE, Mo. (AP)—No sooner had Ken McElroy walked out of the courtroom where they found him guilty of shotgunning the village grocer than, sure enough, there he was back at the B&G tavern.

He showed no remorse. He was sullen. When Ken McElroy was sullen, prudent people gave him room. Even when he was not sullen, tough guys in saloons all across Nodaway County called him mister. It was recognized as unhealthy to cross Ken McElroy.

"He never knelt down to nobody," his young, blonde wife of five years, Trina, reflected the other day. "He didn't care who they were or how many there were. He didn't need nobody beside him."

Just so. He was a big, thickset man of 47 ill-spent years, five-ten and 265 pounds, massive arms, low forehead, bushy eyebrows and sideburns.

He wasn't a street brawler. He was specific. He struck fear in your soul by staring you down, flashing a gun, occasionally using it. If you were his prey for today, he stalked you. He glared at you in silence and when he spoke it was with a slow whisper. Chilling.

He was born on a farm just outside of town. When he was a boy he fell off a hay wagon, requiring a steel plate to be implanted in his head. Some wondered if that was what made him so mean.

This is a small town: 440 people, filling station, bank, post office, tavern, blacktop street, grain elevator. Beyond lie rolling meadows, ripening corn, redwing blackbirds, fat cattle, windmills and silos—a scene off a Sweet Lassy feed calendar.

Ken McElroy jarred that pastoral serenity. So it is with outspoken relief that the citizens of Nodaway County now speak of him in the past tense. He is dead. The fear he brought them, though, still lingers in a new, unexpected form.

At the B&G tavern the day of his conviction, last June 26, he was very much alive, and he was decidedly sullen.

"I been fighting prosecutors since I was 13 years old and I'm damn near 50," he muttered in his beer. "This is the first time I've lost."

For the next two weeks the townspeople muttered, too. They wondered why Ken McElroy was in the B&G tavern in the first place, or anywhere else than they had wanted him to be approximately since he was 13, which was in a well-barred jail.

Here he was again, scot-free on a $40,000 appeal bond, terrorizing the countryside. Bond or no bond, he had swaggered into the B&G tavern toting an M-1 rifle with a bayonet on it.

"Same old story, Lois Bowenkamp said. "Police arrest him, courts let him go." Lois is the wife of Ernest Bowenkamp, known affectionately around town as Bo, the 72-year-old grocer whom McElroy shot in the neck. Bo survived and is back at work.

On the day of a hearing to revoke McElroy's bond for carrying the rifle, July 10, about 60 men gathered downtown. They figured a big crowd at the hearing would impress the judge, and they figured to go to the courthouse together. With McElroy still loose it would not be wise to go singly.

When the men got to town, though, they learned the hearing had been postponed. Another maddening delay. In their frustration they gathered at the Legion hall and invited the sheriff to discuss how to protect themselves from the county menace.

The meeting broke up when someone burst in with a message that more than once had cleared the streets of Skidmore.

"McElroy's in town."

This time they didn't clear the streets. This time they strode over to the B&G, and when McElroy finished his beer, they walked out with him. They stared wordlessly as he got into his pickup. Suddenly, someone put at least three bullets in McElroy's head.

Now a new terror grips the people of Skidmore. Having survived their fear of the lawless, they now fear the law. Not one person in that crowd has been willing to say who it was who shot and killed Ken Rex McElroy.

Trina McElroy, who was with him, told a coroner's jury she saw who it was and named his name. Nonetheless, the jury concluded McElroy was killed by a "person or persons unknown." Now a grand jury in another county will investigate.

Trina was not McElroy's first wife. She was his fourth, the mother of three of the 15 children he fathered over the years.

They were married when their first child was a year old and Trina was 17—married under circumstances the prosecutor termed "suspicious." The townspeople had other words for it.

The prosecutor had charged McElroy with raping Trina. Trina says it was a lie, that they wanted to get married all along. Fair enough, except that Ken already had a wife and, besides, Trina would need her parents' consent, which they refused to give.

A few days before the rape trial four things happened.

One, Ken got a divorce. Two, a house burned down. Three, Trina's parents gave their consent. Four, Ken and Trina found a magistrate in another county who married them. The house that burned down belonged to Trina's parents.

Thus ended the possibility of Trina's testifying against Ken. The rape charges were dropped.

Charges being dropped for lack of people willing to testify against Ken McElroy was the theme of his long criminal record. His lawyer said he had been run in and turned loose "for lack of a case" so many times he couldn't remember them all.

Rustling livestock, threatening people, molesting a minor, arson, you name it, McElroy had been charged with it, but witnesses had a way of backing off. When he was tried for shooting a farmer (who had suggested that McElroy leave his farm and quit shooting pheasants out of season), the witnesses had faulty memories. Not guilty.

So it went, until he shot Bo Bowenkamp. Guilty. Finally.

"Oh, he was intimidating, Lois Bowenkamp said. "You can't know how awful it was. My neighbor and I took turns sleeping at night.

"Before the trial, he would drive up in his pickup at night and sit there. Occasionally he would fire a gun. We knew him, knew his reputation. It was frightening."

You could never know what small thing might set McElroy off. His falling out with Bo Bowenkamp resulted from Bo's clerk asking McElroy's daughter to put back a candy bar she hadn't paid for or, from McElroy's view, "accusing her of raiding the store."

As if shooting Bo over that weren't enough, McElroy got mad at the preacher who visited Bo in the hospital and threatened him, too.

When McElroy roared into town in his pickup with the big mud flaps and the gun rack, his wife in a second pickup ("backup," he explained), sometimes a third pickup, everybody fled not so much for their immediate safety but for fear that they might see McElroy do something they would have to testify to later.

In fairness to the late Ken McElroy, it is also true that, like another who once prowled these parts and met his Maker just south of here, Jesse James, he was suspected of every crime in the county.

Especially rustling. Last year, Nodaway County led the state in stolen livestock—six times the thefts in any other county—and the ranchers who were aware of that were also aware that Ken McElroy always had a pocket full of money.

He lived on a small farm not likely to win any agricultural awards, so where did he get it all? He claimed also to trade in antiques, to which everybody said, but not to his face, whose antiques?

We're talking money. He paid for his pickups in cash. He paid his lawyer in cash. He tossed $8,000 on the bar at the B&G and told the bartender, "If that ain't enough I've got a suitcase full at home." He peeled a hundred-dollar bill off his wad and told Lois Bowenkamp it was hers if she would try to whip Trina on the Skidmore street.

People here are looking to see what happens to the rustling problem now that Ken McElroy is laid in his grave.

It will be more interesting to see what happens to Skidmore.

The McElroy shooting has thoroughly shaken this rural community. The townsfolk don't want to talk just about who might have shot him; they don't want to talk about "the incident," as they refer to it, at all, not even among themselves.

"All we want to do," Lois Bowenkamp said, "is to go back to doing what we do best, which is minding our own business."

For eight years Jules Loh traveled the back roads of America, finding the stories nobody else was reporting and writing them with a voice that was his and only his. His column, "Elsewhere in America," appeared twice a week. Each article was 600 words long. Originally they were 750 words long, but Loh found that editors were cutting off the last couple of paragraphs, and he wanted the last word, so he cut back.

It's not easy doing what Loh did. He was always scrambling. Calvin Trillin wrote the same kinds of stories for the New Yorker; on the infrequent occasions when the two road warriors were in New York at the same time, they would lunch together and trade story ideas: This one is too complicated for 600 words, so you can have it, Bud; this one will never make a New Yorker-length piece, so it's yours, Jules.

"I remember one time I was on the west slope of the Rockies—Mount Rose, Colo., I think was the name of the town," he recalls. "I needed a column that day, and I didn't have one. And the distances are so long. . . . Well, I pulled into a filling station, and the first thing I noticed was that the guy pumping gas was an elderly man, 60s or 70s. Which seemed unusual, but not that unusual. But I was so desperate, I said to him while he was pumping my gas, 'I'm looking for somebody. Who is the nicest person in town?'

"And he said, 'The schoolteacher? Miss So-and-So?'

"I said, 'That's exactly who I mean. Why is she the nicest?'

"He said, 'Oh, everybody thinks she's the nicest person in town.'

"And she was.

"I found her. And she was quite a lady. She taught the first and second grades. They came out and sang 'Oh beautiful for spacious skies' out in the yard, and she had them point to them—there's the spacious skies. 'Purple mountains majesty'—they pointed to that. 'Waves of grain'—they pointed to that. So they had there, in front of their eyes, all the attributes of America, God bless it.

"And then she talked about teaching children and how she made all of them take their shoes off. A local man financed some wall-to-wall carpet for her classroom so that her children could all take their shoes off. She remembered that as a little girl everybody liked to go barefoot. And they did!

"That's the serendipity that you have to rely on every once in a while."

Eight years of looking for the nicest or most interesting or most perplexing person in every town can wear on you. "I was about to go crazy," Loh says. So he quit the column, took a long vacation, and came back to the AP without the tyranny of a twice-weekly column.

The story of Ken Rex McElroy was the first piece he did upon his return. He had seen brief news stories on this killing—nothing much, just the bare-bones facts: "The idea that there were no witnesses to this just intrigued me. How could it be? So I just went out there."

People talked to him, he says, because—well, perhaps it is best to leave the rest to Jules.

"I think that I pursued them more than a spot reporter would. A spot reporter's looking for one or two things. I don't know what I'm looking for. And so I'm looking for talk—just conversation—and whatever comes up. And even the ones who have reason to hate a reporter coming into their life—well, like McElroy's wife. I'd ask her about other things, how she's getting along, how she's handling all this. Do you want to talk to me about it? Well, generally, they'd say no. And I'd say, 'Well, why not?' . . . They would tell me things that they haven't told before. But it's not because they didn't want to—it's because nobody pursued them. . . .

"The grocer, Bo—he and his wife did not want to talk to me. Because they said, 'Look, this is over with. I don't want to talk.' That, of course, was true of everybody except maybe the bartender—the various bartenders. But Bo finally saw that I was not someone to be frightened of. I went back to him two or three times. He told me, 'You ought to talk to so-and-so.' 'You want to talk to somebody? Talk to so-and-so.' And it was always good. I'd come back and say, 'He was very interesting. He told me how this guy used to steal antiques or whatever.' I'd go back to him and ask if he had anybody else to talk to. So I got to know him that way, having him steer me to people to talk to. Finally, it was his wife who did talk."

And yes, McElroy's wife did tell Loh the name of the man she had identified as the killer. But Loh did not use it: "I wasn't sure that she really knew. I'm sure there were legal reasons, but not for that reason, mainly. I couldn't dare to identify somebody and not be positive."

Loh doesn't think of himself as a writer. He grew up in a house full of books; he describes his mother as "very literate," a friend of the writer Flannery O'Connor. As a youth, he read Southern writers like William Faulkner. "I thought to myself, 'I could never do that. But I know that I can outreport anybody. Because that's something you can learn.' I always thought that writers were born but that you could learn to report. And I was just determined that I would do that. Ask all the right questions."

He took up bird-watching, "to make myself an observer. . . . I knew that a bird with red wings was not sufficient. You had to notice more than that to identify it in the bird book."

So when he reported a story, he went in with eyes wide open.

"There were certain things that I tried to include in every story,

whether it was 600 words or 6,000. I always felt that I owed the reader a description of where I am or who I'm talking to."

But he also felt he owed the reader the story under the story, and so he would be persistent in his interviewing—nicely, of course, with a courtly Southern manner.

He remembers the time he trekked to Oregon to interview a woman who wrote articles for Birdwatcher's Digest. When he asked how she became a bird-watcher, she evaded the question.

"Well, you're one," she said. "How did you?"

But Loh pressed the question. "My father and mother were both bird-watchers."

Not enough. "My father got me some binoculars when I was 6, I think."

Finally Loh asked, "Why did you keep on? You're 6 years old, you run and climb trees and play with dolls and so forth. Why did you keep on with bird-watching?"

"Well," she said, "they told me I was going to go blind."

Really, Loh said.

"I had this problem with my eyes, and I had never seen a rufus-sided towhee."

Why did you want to see that bird? asked Loh.

"Only because I hadn't," she said. "And I wanted to stay alive and not be blind until I saw one. And so I kept looking, and I never did see one until finally, I saw one. And I didn't go blind."

And with that, Jules Loh had his story.

After 39 years at the AP, Loh retired. Some of the recent changes in journalism please him—portable computers, for example. He spent years dictating his stories from far-off spots over cranky phone lines to crankier office assistants, and the computer would have been a big help.

He's less enamored of reporters who seek celebrity.

"I was printed in 600, 700 newspapers. . . . But I really cherished my anonymity. There were a lot of people who read it, and I wound up on many refrigerator doors and got a lot of Christmas cards and things like that, but I could still go into any town and be utterly anonymous." He has no plans to go back to work. But if he did, he knows one story he could write—the story he always kept in his back pocket, just in case he was desperate and nothing else appeared.

"Every town, large and small, from any neighborhood in New York to any neighborhood in Mount Rose, Colo., has a coffee shop, a morning coffee shop, where everybody goes. The movers and shakers of the town, all four of them or five, meet there. And they all are similar. There's a quietness about them, only disturbed by the coffee cups and silverware clinking, the rustle of newspapers, where everybody just gets organized, gets the cobwebs out of their brains, gets ready for the day. . . .

"But I never did write that, because I knew I always could."

5 About Writing

Rene J. "Jack" Cappon says Jules Loh is the best reporter he's ever known. "What makes Jules especially good is his eyeballs," Cappon says. Loh sees, and what he sees, he describes. He also has a way of asking questions: "The more obvious answers he gets, the more follow-up questions he asks."

Cappon is the AP's most renowned expert on writing; he's the author of "The Word," still one of the best guides to the craft of putting words together ever written. But ask him what's more important, reporting or writing, and he doesn't hesitate.

"Reporting is the essence of good writing. A well-reported story quite plainly written can be more interesting than the very best style and phrasemaking," Cappon says. "Phrasemaking is really nothing. It's the reporting that really buttresses the story."

First, good reporting focuses the story. If you're examining poverty in a rural county, you can illustrate it by profiling one of the hundreds of poor people who live there.

The challenge is finding the right one.

Saul Pett, a Pulitzer Prize–winning AP reporter, once went to Iowa to write about a farmer as part of a package of stories entitled "Faces of the Nation." After a week he announced that he had found the farmer he would write about. Cappon was incredulous:

Why had it taken Pett a whole week to find a farmer in a state teeming with them?

Pett's answer was that just any farmer wouldn't do. He wanted a farmer who was articulate, dispassionate and authentic. Without a good subject, Pett's considerable writing skills would not have been able to generate a good story.

At the same time, Cappon says, "Good writing depends on the use of specifics, not abstractions. That can only be supplied by the writer. An editor can't make them up."

By specifics, Cappon means "tangible things—houses, cows, whatever." These are the kinds of details with which Ted Anthony and Jules Loh would fill their notebooks, though only a small percentage would find their way into their stories.

"As you report, you really don't know what kind of detail will fit in," Cappon says. Regardless, just by accumulating facts and details, the reporter makes his or her job as a writer easier; if you truly know and understand your subject, you can write more authoritatively, without the need to attribute every bit of the story to experts or others. And that makes a story more readable.

These details also add to the writer's palette. Reporters, Cappon says, should envision themselves as producers of television documentaries. Imagine, he says, a camera panning luxury apartment houses in some exotic foreign place and then focusing on a hovel. Without words, the creator of that documentary has said a lot, purely through what the camera is showing and when; a writer can do the same thing through the adroit manipulation of details.

But only if those details are in his or her notebook.

6 Profiles

An Elderly Woman and the Confounding Gift of Sight

By HELEN O'NEILL
AP National Writer

ENOSBURG FALLS, Vt. (AP)—If Eva Suggs could, she would paint the world purple. She would live in a purple house and sleep on a purple pillow and drive a purple car. Sometimes, she would permit other colors into her world, but they would have to be bright, really bright, like the cherry-red barns that dot the Vermont countryside, so pretty beneath the great blue sky and the green hills that seem to roll forever.

Eva chuckles. She knows the most she will ever have is a purple dress. But an old lady can dream.

And now she can see.

Eva was born blind, victim of a rare genetic corneal defect that was passed on from her paternal grandfather, and that she, in turn, passed on to her children and their children and their children. A year ago she received what she calls her great gift—an operation that gave her sight.

After nearly 80 years of fumbling about in a colorless world, Eva can march down the pale yellow corridors of her rest home without touching the walls. She can revel in the twirl of a blue and gold dress. She can thrill at the way Felix the cat turns drowsily toward her when she calls his name. She can sneak delicious glances in the mirror to fix her hair.

"My sight," Eva says joyfully, "is a gift from God."

God's gift has already fulfilled her most treasured dream—to see photographs of her parents before she dies. And it has let her gaze into the beautiful brown eyes of 2-year-old Renee, who, at 4 months, had the same eye surgery as her great grandmother.

But Eva's gift came with its own set of obligations and questions and worries. The world seems to expect so much now that she no longer leans on her red and white cane. Eva expects so much of herself.

Her vision is far from perfect. By most standards she is legally blind—a notion that seems ridiculous to Eva as she proudly reads aloud the biggest letters on the doctor's chart, or points out the color of a car.

Eva knows that blindness has sheltered her from more than the light. It shut her off from decisions, like what clothes to wear or where to hang pictures on the wall. It shut her off from an education, from a cluttered mind.

She worries about falling. She worries about losing her gift and being suddenly thrust back into darkness. Most of all she worries about her place in this dazzling world of daylight, where reds and yellows and golds glisten in the sun.

* * *

Eva is nervous. She fusses about her room, straightening her dress, touching up her hair, lingering in the comfort of the drawn shades. Finally, she takes a deep breath and steps into the light.

This sunny afternoon is a big one. Eva is taking her first stroll down Main Street. Her steps are labored, her gait hesitant. At times she looks frightened and lost. "It's exciting," Eva says gamely, her pale greenish-blue eyes watering in the glare.

She refuses to wear the thick black glasses the doctor gave her. Not here, not on Main Street, not where she might meet someone she knows. No, Eva wants to walk down the street and nod at neighbors and smile her good mornings to the world.

But every step brings confusion.

Eva has no idea why there are so many cheerfully decorated banners flapping outside the stores. Sure, they look pretty, but aren't they supposed to signify something, like a parade or a holiday? Surely store owners don't just hang them out for decoration.

"There must be something on," she concludes.

The clothes store is enticing, but there are three wooden steps outside. Steps are a crisis. They swirl before her, a blur of crisscrossing lines. She has no idea how high they are, how low, how far apart. She misses her cane.

In the window of a children's store, her eyes settle on a poster of Winnie-the-Pooh. Eva grew up on an isolated farm near the Canadian border. The only bears she knows of are wild ones. She has no idea what to make of this tubby little creature with his honey pot. Disconcerted, she moves on.

A yellow sports car screeches to a halt at the stop sign, its radio pounding loud enough to make the pavement pulse.

"Just like a band," Eva says, beaming at the two youths inside. They throw bored, disdainful glances her way. Eva is thrilled. She can't get over the ever-changing expressions on the faces of strangers.

* * *

The youths roar off and return a few minutes later. Eva smiles at them again.

Eva grew up on Isle La Motte, a tiny

island on Lake Champlain, dotted with cornfields and apple orchards, drenched in a beauty that as a child she could only feel.

Eva doesn't need her eyes to find her way to the small brown farmhouse where her parents raised 14 children. The smell of the shore, the rustle of the trees, the feel of the road tell her she is home.

"Isn't it pretty," she says, her eyes confirming the image she always carried in her head.

It's her first trip back in years and, for now, memories are stronger than sight: the sound of her sisters teasing her for being afraid of cows, the gentle touch of her mother guiding her hands as she teaches her to bake a cake, the worried tone of her father as he tells her cannot go to school.

Her family was poor. Her father worked another man's farm, milked another man's cows. Eva would help, herding cows, picking raspberries, scrubbing floors while her brothers and sisters went to school. Eva, the sixth child, was the only one born blind.

"Pa protected me," she says. "He didn't let me leave the house. No boyfriends for me."

When her father died, her mother moved the family to Alburg, a tiny town on the Canadian border about seven miles away. Eva met Ward Washburn when he came to deliver wood one day.

Eva talks of their marriage as one of convenience: She needed someone to take care of her, and Ward had just built a house. They lived together for about 30 years, raising two children, Lawrence and Shirley. The children went to a boarding school for the blind in Boston when they were seven, and Eva rarely had contact with them after that.

Today Lawrence's daughter Michelle Willard lives in Eva's old house, along with her husband, Shawn, and their daughters, Danielle, 4, and Renee, 2.

Michelle inherited her grandmother's spunk along with her bad eyes. It was she who persuaded Eva to undergo corneal transplant operations at the age of 78. The surgery, a relatively simple procedure, had been available for years. But no one had ever told Eva about it, and at first she was afraid.

Little Renee convinced her. If the baby's eyes could be opened up to the world, why not those of her great-grandmother?

Eva is mesmerized by Renee. She follows the toddler everywhere, soaking up every expression, every glance.

"Look at her, she's so cute," Eva cries, as she hugs the wriggling child and wonders, for the first time, what her own children looked like at that age.

Renee's eyes, perfect brown buttons, fascinate Eva most of all. Months after the child was born, her corneas, the transparent tissue that covers the iris and pupil, began rapidly turning a dull gray. The family curse. The medical term for their blindness is congenital corneal dystrophy. Doctors say they have rarely seen anything like it.

In the kitchen Eva and Michelle talk about the child, about the chances she will have, about their own eyes and the rogue gene that swims through their family gene-pool.

Michelle produces photographs of her father and Eva's son—Lawrence—a strong, handsome man with crooked eyes and a shy smile. Eva pores over them sadly. It's hard to look at pictures of her children and not feel guilty.

"Grandma, there were good times too," Michelle says.

Eva shakes her head. She worries that she wasn't a good enough mother, worries that is why Shirley died in her late 30s, and Lawrence killed himself at 43.

The suicide came seven years after the operation that gave him sight, and the family has always wondered. Did he choose to die because he couldn't cope? Others, overwhelmed by the sudden gift of vision, have made that choice.

Eva is vague about these and other details of her life she doesn't want to talk about. She left Ward in the early 1970s and spent the next two decades in a home for the blind in North Carolina. There, she learned skills for the first time: Braille, typing, crochet. And she was married again, to a blind resident named Frederick Suggs, who died of cancer shortly after their wedding.

In 1995 her sisters paid for her ticket back to Vermont. Two years later Michelle took her to Dr. William Eichner for the first time.

* * *

The nurses teased Eva about how it was "love at first sight" when they removed the bandages and she gazed into Dr. Eichner's eyes. In fact, Eva remembers a dizzying confusion of light, more brilliant than she could have imagined.

"Daylight," she thought. "So this is what it looks like."

Gradually, the light gave way to shapes, to a world that was far more cluttered than she had believed. The operations—one on each eye—took place six months apart, in July 1997 and January 1998. During the surgeries, which each lasted about an hour, Dr. Eichner removed the bad corneas and stitched in new ones from an eye bank. He describes it as replacing windows that were blacked out with ones that are clear.

Eva spent a night in the hospital after each operation. Then she was driven back to the rest home.

Alone in her room, Eva tried to sort through the emotions and colors swimming around in her head. I'm not handicapped anymore, she kept thinking. I can see like a normal person.

But what was normal? Was this the way others viewed the world, this chaotic jumble of doors and windows and colors and cars? Eva was given no brochures to guide her, no advice on how to cope.

But Eva knew exactly what to do. She knelt before the crucifix above her bed and said a prayer of thanks. Then she took out photographs of her parents and stared at them for a long, long time.

Her father looked skinnier than she had imagined, her mother heavier.

And her own reflection: That was the most intriguing image of all. In a handheld mirror she examined her face, touching her soft brown curls, tracing her fingers over her lips when she smiled, stroking her cheeks. She liked what she saw. Except for the wrinkles. "My skin was much more smooth before the operation," she says.

Even Dr. Eichner is surprised by the relative ease with which Eva has adjusted to sight. Tests had shown her to be totally blind, not able to distinguish any difference between light and dark. Today she can read if the print is large enough.

Eva says it is not hard to master letters after learning the alphabet by touch. Distance is much more difficult. She doesn't understand foreground and background. She is startled by the constant shifting of her shadow.

From the window in her room, Eva can see a river and a farm at the other side. But she has no sense of how far away they are. She sees cows in the field, but she has no idea if there are 100 or 500.

Eva knows these are things that her eyes might never learn. She professes not to care.

"I'm just going to see all that I can," she says, "and not worry about what I have missed."

Eva spends her days sitting in her room, gazing at the river and her photographs. Her talking watch announces when it is time for lunch and bingo and Mass.

She longs for a Bible with letters large enough to read. She fantasizes about going to Hollywood and seeing the faces of the stars, especially Dolly Parton, the prettiest one. She would love to see a moose. She says she would be content, now that she has seen a bit of the world, to close her eyes and die. She is ready to see her parents in heaven.

"How do you know there is a heaven?" asks an old man as they sit on the rest home porch and discuss God's gift. "You can't see it. You can't see God."

"But I can see all his creations," Eva says.

She clicks her fingers and leans toward the home's pet dog, a golden Belgian shepherd. "Here, Beauty," she calls. "Come here, Beauty."

Old and lame and a little blind himself, Beauty shuffles over and nuzzles her hand.

Michelle Willard could not understand why anyone would want to write an article about her grandmother. To Willard, Eva Suggs was a selfish, embittered old woman who couldn't cope with life, who didn't appreciate the great gift she had received— the gift of sight.

But Helen O'Neill was determined. She was certain that there was a great story in Eva Suggs, an 80-year-old woman who had been blind from birth and suddenly had gained her vision. She was certain, though she knew that Eva would not be a voluble subject— she had had little education and had been shunted from one institution to another. She was certain, though when she called Eva for the first time, the old woman did little but complain about her loneliness.

"On the phone, I remember thinking, 'Oh, God.' And I know other journalists thought the same thing because others called her and never did a story. Because she's not terribly articulate. But you know, there's all this stuff in there, and she's got all these thoughts about things." The challenge, O'Neill says, was to find some way to get those thoughts out.

She had heard about Eva while chatting with friends at a wedding. They mentioned this old woman and her new sight. "I'm just a chatterbox," she says. "I don't think I do it consciously . . . but as soon as somebody says something, I say, 'That could be a good story.' "

But when she thought about Eva's story, she realized that she did not know enough about blindness and about sight to ask the right questions of someone with Eva's singular experience.

She contacted several organizations for the blind, trying to find others who had suddenly received their sight. She read books on blindness and searched for sources on the Web.

Her research led her to Melanie Brunson, a staffer at the American Council of the Blind. Brunson has been blind all her life and is married to a man whose occupation is dependent on seeing—he's a photographer. They have had long conversations about sight; he has tried to explain color, space, perspective. But try as she might, she can't really understand those concepts. "She needs to physically 'feel' something in order to make sense of it," O'Neill says.

Brunson is not quoted in the story O'Neill wrote about Eva Suggs. But she is there, in the underpinnings of O'Neill's reporting. Without the insight provided by this blind woman, O'Neill would not have been able to put herself in the place of Eva, a woman who suddenly was given a fifth sense.

This is important, because Helen O'Neill gets so close to her subjects that sometimes you would swear that you can see the pores in their skin. She has written about a young scientist who died horribly after her hand touched a drop of mercury. She has written about a woman who identified her rapist with absolute certainty only to learn, years later, that DNA testing had proved her wrong. She has written about a politician so profoundly handicapped that his head is perched on an entirely useless body. Always she writes with a deep sense of empathy and understanding that is achieved only through painstaking reporting.

When O'Neill arrived in Vermont, she found Eva sitting in her sparsely furnished bedroom at the nursing home, where she gazed at a photograph of her parents or at a distant field outside her window.

"What struck me most was her loneliness," O'Neill says. "It was so real and so raw. It was clear that her great gift of sight hadn't solved her biggest problem: She was just as unhappy as when she was blind. Her sight wasn't good enough for her to go out on her own, and anyway, she had nowhere to go. Main Street was too far away. She also had absolutely no money to spend. She kept saying that she had nothing left to live for, she just wanted to die."

But O'Neill spent several days with Eva, taking her out to lunch, walking her through town, watching her reaction to things: human expressions, shop windows, steps. She saw delight, but she also saw fear; Eva was scared of the unknown and missed the sightless world she had inhabited for so long.

She took Eva for a drive to the little island where she had grown up, about an hour away. O'Neill watched as Eva found her way unerringly to a place she had never seen. But when they arrived, Eva just smiled nervously and asked to go back to the nursing home.

Gradually Eva opened up. She took a liking to Tony Talbot, the photographer who was working with O'Neill. "He treated her as if she was the most important assignment he'd ever worked on," O'Neill recalls. "He made her feel like a star, and she loved it. It made her open up more to me."

Says Talbot: "Sometimes I can act as a bridge between the reporter and the subject. Sometimes I can help the reporter see the person in a different way."

O'Neill went to see Eva's granddaughter, Michelle, and learned more about Eva's life, her daughter's death and her son's suicide. Eva had lived in this house years before, with her husband; the next day O'Neill drove her to Michelle's house, and there—in a familiar setting—Eva talked more openly about some of the sadder episodes in her life.

O'Neill does not prepare for interviews by compiling a list of questions.

"Sometimes I'll write a few little notes to myself to remember some really key points that I want to ask, particularly if it's something very sensitive. But very minor, just a couple of jots in my notebook," she says. "And other than that, I just let it all flow. I just really have a conversation. I don't interview."

She tries to limit the length of these conversations: "I think people can only talk for a certain length of time. It's just too exhausting. So I think it's really helpful to go out to dinner or go somewhere and do something. But I like to start or end in their homes, because I like to see them at home. . . .

"And I think that part of the conversation is revealing a little bit about yourself as well, particularly if you're asking them intimate details of their life—I think you have to be prepared to reveal some of the things in your life, too."

Not that she expects an answer to all her questions: "The story I'm working on, I asked a very personal question, and she said, 'I won't go there. I refuse to talk about it.' Actually, she said that to me twice. I think you deal with it the way you deal with everything else as a human being. You follow your instincts. Apologize if you have to apologize, but I think you have to ask hard personal questions.

"That is another way of keeping the boundaries. You're there with your notebook asking the questions. You don't not ask the question because you're worried about upsetting somebody. You have to figure out the way to ask it."

Each day, when she left Eva, she would type some notes, "not in great depth. More just thoughts in my head. Not about the story, but what I was observing. Little things so I'll be able to remember, so I'll be able to bring myself back to where I was, to this setting. And sometimes I'll ask someone to talk into a tape recorder. I don't tape interviews, but I just want to remember their voices. If they say anything, even read a piece, the voice will sort of remind me of the feeling I had when I was in the room with them."

She doesn't worry much about writing down every word her subject says; in fact, she doesn't use a lot of quotes in her stories.

"As a younger reporter, I think you use a lot more quotes, and I think a lot of them are filler," she says. "As you get older and do real storytelling, you find you only need something if it's really wonderful. Otherwise, usually there's a more wonderful way to say it."

Instead, she fills her notebook with detail—the color of someone's clothes, the way in which he is sitting—though she knows that it is unlikely that most of it will find its way into her story. In the middle of an interview she often realizes that she neglected to get the color of his eyes and finds herself juggling questions and answers while trying to determine if this guy has hazel or brown peepers.

She doesn't write while reporting—"I prefer to immerse myself in something and just come out the other end and really think about it when I write the story"—but sometimes she will scribble down a phrase or even a paragraph that comes to her while she's driving. The ending to Eva's story, though, was obvious from the moment she saw the old man and the dog a few minutes before she left for home.

"It was so crystal clear," she says.

She knows that she has the luxury of time, more time to report, to think, and to write than most reporters have, but she feels there is no other way to write these stories. She is known to agonize over her work. It comes with the territory; she often becomes intimately involved with her subjects, and so she worries about how they will be depicted in her stories and whether she is exploiting them or their sorrows.

"I think if you're doing the kinds of profiles that I'm doing, you have to be empathetic. It has to be genuine or people will know. And it is," she says.

When she was working on the story about the scientist who succumbed to mercury poisoning and the victim's husband called, out of his mind with worry about the way that her death would be portrayed, O'Neill made another trip to New Hampshire—purely to reassure him.

And when she wrote about a family's desperate effort to find its son and brother—tragically, he had died of a fall in a desert canyon—the youth's father allowed her to accompany him on a pilgrimage to the spot where the boy had died. The father intended to plant a cross in the rock where the young man had hit his head, but when he arrived there, he found that his son had hit his head on a ponderosa pine, not a stone.

"He just lost it. He was sobbing, what should he do now?" O'Neill recalls.

"And I said, 'Why don't you just carve a cross into the tree?' "

He did. And O'Neill wondered for a long time: Had she overstepped the bounds of objectivity? Eventually she decided she had not: "At that moment I just thought it was the compassionate thing to do."

There was no agony in writing Eva's story. She knew that Eva would love it. She spent several days in Vermont and then a week writing; the first draft was substantially unchanged. And when the story appeared, both Helen and Eva received phone calls from around the country. O'Neill had written about Eva's simple desires—for a large-print Bible and purple sheets—and now the nursing home was inundated with sheets and Bibles, so many that it had to donate them to local charities.

The best response, though, came from Eva's granddaughter, Michelle.

"Your article painted a beautiful portrait of my grandmother," she wrote in a letter to O'Neill. "I have to confess, you spent more time with her than I have in my entire life. That sounds very strange to me. I read the article three times today, and it is only now that I have become aware of how little I know about her. To be sheltered from the world in every way must have been very difficult for her. . . .

"I have heard stories about her my whole life—tales of a bitter, vindictive woman who loved to stir up trouble. While I am sure that many of these recollections contain a degree of truth, I am also sure that Grandma felt very cheated by the world in general."

O'Neill's work—the archaeological effort she put into understanding Eva's life—had made Michelle appreciate her grandmother. She would visit Eva more often, bring Eva into her life.

"I think that is all that Eva ever wanted," O'Neill says.

7 The Art of the Sit-Down Interview

Jane Fonda Talks, and Talks Some More

By HILLEL ITALIE
Associated Press Writer

NEW YORK (AP)—The ground rules are less than promising: no acting questions, no personal questions and, if you value your life, no mention of Vietnam. Today, Jane Fonda has just one item on her agenda.

"As you know, Jane will only talk about fitness," a representative of her video distributor says cheerfully on the elevator ride up to Fonda's hotel suite. "But if she feels relaxed, she might open about other subjects. You might get her to talk about Ted and fishing."

Fighting back images of Ted Turner cleaning a rainbow trout, we get off at the 36th floor and are greeted at the door by Fonda, who shakes hands and briefly excuses herself to finish another interview. She seems rushed—later this morning she is to help her son, Troy, move in to his apartment. But she's upbeat, friendly.

A few minutes later, Fonda settles into a small armchair and rests her legs on a glass coffee table. She is wearing a black, buttoned blouse and gray pants. Her auburn hair falls to her shoulders; her fingers are long and slender. Her feet are bare; her toenails painted red.

Fonda is 55, but the magic number today is 10 million, as in total video sales since she kicked off—literally—the video exercise boom in 1982. There also have been eight audiotapes, total sales of more than 2 million, and a best-selling workout book.

New product is being developed all the time, with three new tapes coming out this fall: "Jane Fonda's Pregnancy Workout," "Jane Fonda's Start Up" and "Jane Fonda's Favorite Fat Burners," a compilation of four previous workouts.

"A lot of it has to do with my need to create boundaries," Fonda says of her motivation behind exercising. "I tend to be like a lot of women—someone who forgets myself. . . . And I'll find myself lost somewhere out there, trying to please everyone. Exercise helps me define myself."

This leads, oh so gently, to acting, which Fonda says had the effect of making her lose touch with herself. The intensity she brought to her work caused "mini-breakdowns" before each film began. It may have been the reason she finally gave it up.

"It was like, you're not quite the character yet, but you're not yourself fully, anymore," she says of the weeks leading up to filming. "It was horrible; it was always absolutely horrible. I would hate myself. . . .

"And when the movie would be over—abject sadness and melancholy, just horrible depression. I think that's true for many actors. You live for someone else and in between, it's like, 'Who am I?' . . . Before I met Ted and decided I didn't want to act anymore, I was already not wanting to act anymore."

These days, her heart clearly is in physical fitness. She describes the months-long process involved with constructing the workouts, the give and take over music and sets and exercises. It recalls the development of a feature film.

The videos—and fitness in general—have been an education for Fonda. Her first tape was criticized for having a routine so intense it was potentially dangerous. Earlier this year, she confessed to Family Circle magazine she was once hooked on exercise, working out four hours a day.

"I'm a pretty compulsive kind of person," she says, "and for a long time I suffered from eating disorders. Exercising helped me to recover from that, but not all by itself. I had to teach myself balance and moderation; that didn't come to me naturally."

Fonda admits that 20 years ago she never thought she'd be living like this: workout tapes, retired from acting, the adoring wife of a wealthy businessman. She is as likely to be seen rooting on the Atlanta Braves as she is to be marching in a political rally. Young fans of her videos might find it hard to imagine that the friendly instructor chanting "work those thighs" once had her address book Xeroxed by government agents.

"I don't call it conservative," she says of her current politics. "I've gotten smarter, I've gotten more compassionate. I've gotten less impatient. I have learned through bitter experience that life is not simple, black and white and all that.

"The fact is there's nothing wrong when you're young and seeing things in black and white. If they don't do it, who will? Somebody has to man the barricades—that's a function of youth, the pure idealism and the willingness to die for your ideals."

She was supposed to talk about fitness, but the past proves irresistible, like chocolate cake waved under her nose. Fonda notes her most challenging roles often were related to the times in which the films were made. There was "They Shoot Horses, Don't They?" It was released in 1969, just as she was becoming politicized about Vietnam. Two years later came "Klute," bringing Fonda an Academy Award and her first feminist education.

"I had just done 'Barbarella,' and it was not politically correct and I was worried about it. . . . So here I was supposed to be playing this hooker and I didn't know how to do it in a way to get respect, and then I just started getting into her," she recalls.

"Something in my heart as Bree Daniel opened up to other women, that's what led to the scene . . . where I'm finally with the guy when he puts the tape recorder down and he starts to play it, and I can hear the voice of the girlfriend who has been killed, and I realized this is the guy and he's going to kill me.

"I spent weeks with hookers and call girls and streetwalkers and I had gone through the morgue and had looked through the pictures and when I heard the tape, I cried one tear and my nose started running. It was totally unprepared, but it was a heart opening to the women who had been the victims of violence. That to me is like the first concrete example of how politics is really about conscience and expanded conscience so you can view people with more empathy."

Still, she hardly sounds like an alumna of Nixon's Enemies List when asked how she reconciles her personal wealth with her political ideals: "If you feel bad about making money, stop making

money, for heaven's sake. I LOVE making money."

Fonda says at first she didn't want to make the videos, fearing they'd hurt her acting career. But she changed her mind after receiving letters from women of all ages thanking her for giving them confidence, even for saving their lives.

This leads to another question: Don't men work out to her videos?

"Men don't do 'em," she answers firmly. "I did a video, just a draft of a video. I decided to do an aerobic video based on all the moves guys do in high school, dribbling, all sports related."

But a marketing test revealed that the men wouldn't be interested in pursuing it.

"They felt stupid, putting videos on and having their kids and their wives there," Fonda said. "Your culture is working out at a gym. It's sports, team sports. It's not our culture, for the most part. It's more natural for us to do that; we're at home, anyway."

Women are at home, anyway?

"A lot of women who do the tape are at home with their children and the children do the tapes with them."

Don't men stay at home with the children?

"I'm not saying they don't, but men just don't do videos."

What about Turner?

"He works out in a gym and I work out in a gym, and together we bike ride and we hike and we ski and go for walks and things like that. He's happy enough that I'm continuing to do the videos—I don't have to ask for money," she says with a laugh.

But does he do videos?

"He might do the one I'm going to do in a month or so, but up to now, no. He wouldn't do an aerobics video, it's not his thing."

She pauses and smiles, blushing slightly.

"He likes to look at 'em sometimes; he likes to look at the covers."

When Hillel Italie set out to do a story on Jane Fonda, he did not have days to shadow the star, jetting with her around the country to homes in Atlanta and Montana. He did not have the opportunity to talk with her directors, her family, her closest friends. She was not eager to bare her soul.

No. All he had was an hourlong interview in a Manhattan hotel set up by Fonda's public relations people, who were eager to promote an exercise video.

In the best of all worlds, reporters always would have the luxuries of time and total access to their subjects. In the real world, these things are truly luxuries. Some magazine writers jet around and spend weeks with the people they're writing about, but most reporters must be content with the 1 p.m. slot on Wednesday, just after the crew from WZZZ-TV and before the entertainment writer from the Daily Bugle.

These stories can be superficial fluff, but they don't have to be. There is an art to the sit-down interview. Italie has interviewed writers from Norman Mailer to Laurent de Brunhoff (author of the Babar books), actors from Katharine Hepburn to Robin Williams, musicians from the Bee Gees to Sonic Youth. He has interviewed some of them more than once, although they almost never remember him.

He remembers something Nate Polowetzky, a legendary editor at the AP, once told him, the plaint of a reporter who did many such interviews: "I've known many famous people, but they did not know me."

"If you go in there wanting to be their friend, you're in trouble," Italie says. "At least three-quarters of the time it's a truly enjoyable exchange. Really pleasurable, and you come out of there saying, 'I really enjoyed that.' But if you think you're going to get a Christmas card from them, you'll be fortunate if they remember you the next time you have reason to talk to them."

He had in fact interviewed Fonda once before, when she had been in a movie. Four years had passed, and as usual, the star did not remember him. "I also pretended we never met. To mention it seemed pointless. It's not like we had some deep personal exchange."

The publicist had laid down certain ground rules. This was to be an interview about the video. No questions about movies or about politics. Later, in the elevator on the way to Fonda's room, an assistant to the publicist made one small concession. He didn't have to confine himself to questions about the video. He could also ask about her husband, Ted Turner's, passion for fishing.

The problem was that Italie had no interest in writing a story about trout or about Fonda's latest enterprise. He figured he would try to get Fonda to talk about movies. If she did, fine. If she didn't, he would write either a short celebrity item or nothing at all.

He needed an icebreaker, Often, when he talks with film people, he mentions that he recently saw one of their more obscure works. He remembers interviewing Danny Aiello at the end of a long day in which the actor was promoting a film in which he played Jack Ruby, the killer of John F. Kennedy's assassin, Lee Harvey Oswald.

"You could tell that he had been asked the same questions over and over and over again, and he was almost in a robotic mode. I just came in and shook his hand

and said, 'Hey, I just saw "Bang the Drum Slowly" on TV the other night'—which I had—and he said, 'Oh, that was my first movie.' So I asked, 'What was that like?' And he just starts talking about it. I wasn't necessarily even going to use it. But it's almost like his brain is in operation again, so from there you're getting a whole other level of answers. You're making them think on their feet."

So when he sat down across a coffee table from Jane Fonda, Italie mentioned that he had just seen "The Moon's Our Home," a 1936 comedy starring Margaret Sullavan and her father, Henry Fonda, that was co-written by Dorothy Parker. Jane lit up. She had never seen the film and wrote down the title.

"There was no way that anyone had begun a conversation with her by saying, 'Hey, I just saw "The Moon's Our Home," ' " Italie says. Instead of dropping the name of some well-known Jane Fonda film—something like "Klute" or "Julia"—he showed her that he was really familiar with her world. And he was certain to elicit more than the "bored, canned response" he would get otherwise.

It certainly worked with Jane Fonda. She broke every rule her publicist had set.

"Publicists are really funny. Virtually all the rules they set up are ones that the actor or the author doesn't really want. It's the publicists themselves who are really worried, because they want the product to be sold. Jane Fonda was a case of someone who needed protection from herself."

Once you got Jane Fonda started talking about movies, Italie found, "you couldn't stop her." Most of the interview was devoted to film, though she also talked about Vietnam and its effect on her career. "Supposedly, Vietnam was a big taboo: 'You don't bring up Vietnam with her.' And SHE brought it up."

Italie did not go in with a list of questions to ask. Like Helen O'Neill, he almost never does. "Almost always the best quotes in a story come from things that simply develop in conversation. You have to be really well prepared—you have to be able to dig to the heart of their work and be able to go wherever they take you. . . . Once you have that, it's hard to do a bad interview. It really is. There just should be so

much to talk about. Whether you want to have questions prepared for yourself, it depends on what makes you feel comfortable. I just know one or two questions that I want to ask, and maybe there are one or two others that I hope will come up during the conversation."

He does not save his toughest question for last, as some reporters do.

"You save it for the right moment. I always feel like the thing you have to do if you're doing an interview is never close yourself off to anything. Always be ready for a sudden change. If you sort of burrow your head down and ask questions, then you're getting a very different kind of interview. Maybe the person will say something that opens the door. But obviously, if that doesn't happen, the thing to do is, at the end of the interview, say, 'By the way, why did you leave your wife of 40 years for your secretary?' "

When Italie interviewed Fonda the first time, her niece had just been arrested on drug charges, and he was compelled to ask about it. "You'll generally say to them, 'Look, I know you've been asked this, but I've got to do it.' You've sort of got to become their co-conspirator: 'I know this is stupid, but look, can you just give me a comment about what happened with your niece?' Generally, they'll be reasonable with it and say something to you. And sometimes if they sense that you realize that it's an uncomfortable position, they will, ironically, even be more open with you. They won't feel so threatened by it."

Still, he finds that the "further you get away from their work, the more likely they are to lie to you. The closer you get to their work, the more likely they are to tell the truth. Public people lie about their private lives constantly; the examples of people who talk about how much they love their wives and then a week later announce they're divorcing are countless. I just had it happen to me. A year ago I did this piece about (writer) Salman Rushdie, and in it he was going on and on about how happy and settled in he is in his domestic life. Two weeks later there are these articles—he's running around with this young model.

"But they never, ever lie about their work. I've never had somebody not give the truth about the work, about how they felt about their work, about the process of their work, about if you bring up something that seems to be a theme in their work. That's when you get the truth out of them. When you're looking to tell you how they feel about their spouses, you ought to be careful, because it's extremely likely that they're not going to give you the truth; they're just going to be more protective. But about their work, almost to a one, they're quite naked. It's all out there."

Italie does not believe there are bad interview subjects. Artists pegged as bad interviews, he says, are just people who won't put up with stupid questions. While preparing to write about Paul Newman, Italie read a piece in a New York newspaper that bad-mouthed the actor: "Boy, there goes that Paul Newman again; he just won't cooperate." But the paper also ran a transcript of Newman's news conference: "And they were the most inane questions. It was like, 'Are your eyes really blue?' 'How do you stay so handsome?' And of course, he was telling them all to stuff it. And thus, in their minds, he was just a bad interview."

There are some tough interviews, such as the writer Philip Roth. "If you give him any leeway, if there's any stupidity in that question at all, he will zero in on it and go after you. He's fair, though. If you ask him a good question, he answers it. And he gives a good answer." Another writer, V. S. Naipaul, also is renowned as a tough interview; in fact, some years ago, it is said, he reduced another AP reporter to tears. Italie read all of his work, went into the interview with precise questions, and offered no small talk. "It was almost like a business meeting. . . . He gave wonderful answers—all you could ask for—and when it was over, he said, 'Okay, is that enough?' I said, 'That's fine.' " They shook hands and said goodbye.

Again, so much depends on the questions you ask.

"Actually, on the one hand you can say they've been 'asked everything,' but usually they've been asked almost nothing. They've been asked an astonishingly narrow range of questions over and over again. They come to expect it. They're almost on autopilot. . . . All you've got to do is do the research. It's probably easier with

authors than with actors, but just know their work. Because the work tells you what you want to ask them. You really often have an astonishing advantage over the person you're interviewing because you know an incredible amount about them, just from their work. . . . They don't know you, and you know them. You can really get to the heart of things pretty quickly, especially if it's a good artist, because they've really revealed themselves already through their work. And it's just a matter of getting them to articulate that."

Italie says research is half of the interviewer's job—"out of simple respect you owe it to the subject." The other half, he says, is psychological preparation: "There are two things to keep in mind when talking to artists: One, they're like everybody else. Two, they're not like everyone else.

"By this I mean they're all human, flawed, conflicted. . . . If you treat someone like an icon, you're telling less than half the story. The more relaxed about it you are, the more they are. Forgive their failings, but don't ignore them.

"At the same time, don't kid

yourself that they're just plain folks. Artists from all fields have one thing in common: ambition, nonstop ambition. I don't mean this in a bad way. The ambition to write a great book is a wonderful thing, but it changes how you deal with the rest of the world. A lot of people get pushed aside."

The really famous artists, says Italie, "live quite differently from me and you. They don't stand in lines. They don't ride on the subway. They're the center of attention—always. They're aware that everything they say and do will be remembered, scrutinized. The only time I've felt like that was on my wedding day. Being famous is like getting married every day of your life."

There have been reporters who goad celebrities until they are thrown out of hotel rooms and then write about it. Italie isn't into "gotcha" journalism. When he interviewed a first-time writer who did not know how to deal with the press, he found himself feeling protective. "Look," he told her, "do you want to take a moment to say it again?" He did not feel that way about Jane Fonda, though at one point—deep in a conversation that was not about fishing or her video—she looked at him and said, "I really shouldn't be talking about this. You'll help me, right? I don't want to look bad."

He said he would see what he could do. And he feels his story was a fair one.

Unlike the young writer, he says, "Jane Fonda has been around the block hundreds of times. She knows what she's doing."

8 General Assignment or Specialization?

In a span of several weeks, Marcia Dunn wrote stories about the space shuttle and the international space station. She wrote about a rich American's efforts to buy a seat on a spaceship and about the status of women in space. She went to Russia to cover a launch.

In the same time period Larry McShane helped cover the trial of rap artist Sean "Puffy" Combs. He wrote stories about winter weather, about New York City Mayor Rudolph Giuliani, about a strike by workers in a sugar factory. He went to Boston to write a story about the fugitive mobster James "Whitey" Bulger.

Dunn is the AP's aerospace writer; she has covered the space program as a beat since 1990. McShane is a general assignment reporter in the AP's New York City bureau.

They are both among the very best at what they do, but what they do is in some ways very different. Dunn has developed an area of expertise, with a full Rolodex of sources. Every day she follows developments in the space program, working hard to ensure that when something happens, the AP has it first and that the stories are complete and easy to understand.

She was a general assignment reporter in Pittsburgh, but even when she filed high school sports scores and wrote about city affairs, she was developing a specialty in medical reporting.

"I really had a desire to make contacts and follow something thoroughly," she says. "There's such satisfaction in that. I really had the urge to become a so-called expert in one area and just write the heck out of it."

She knew nothing about space when she took the aerospace beat. "It's really pretty specialized, with a lot of acronyms, a lot of engineering stuff, and I had to work hard at that," she says, because engineers are "pretty leery of talking to reporters who don't even know which way the shuttle is pointed."

Space never bores her.

"Even though it sounds like, day to day, the stories are the same—there's another shuttle going up, and they're going back to the space station, and many of the people are the same faces—there's always something new. It's never routine, as NASA likes to say: There's always a new problem with a new part of the shuttle, there's always a new angle to take, a new tactic, and what really is interesting and appealing to me is every day, you can't anticipate what the day will bring."

That is precisely what appeals to McShane about general assignment: "coming in to do something different every day." He recalls the aftermath of the 1993 bombing of the World Trade Center, when he and everyone else in the bureau wrote story after story about the explosion. "After four weeks of that," he says, "it's like banging your head against the wall."

He prefers a "nice mix." One week's work: Friday, in Boston for the Whitey Bulger story. Saturday, covering the funeral of black separatist Khallid Muhammed. Off Sunday and Monday. Tuesday, interviewing multimillionaire Abe Hirschfeld at the Rikers Island jail. Wednesday and Thursday, writing in the office. Friday, the Combs trial.

He has developed some areas of expertise. He has written about organized crime, and he often is assigned light stories because of his writer's touch and sense of humor. But he cannot imagine taking on a beat full time; it would bore him. He does not fear being thrown into a story that he knows nothing about. In fact, he kind of likes it.

"If you know the right people to talk to, or you can find out relatively quickly, it really doesn't matter what you're writing about," he says. "The challenge is to make yourself an expert on whatever it is that day."

Still, there are more beat reporters than ever before both at the AP and elsewhere. Beat reporting brings "an expertise to your subject that makes your story add something to the dialogue, to the understanding," says Lou Boccardi, the AP's president.

It's a necessity. Imagine, for example, sending a general assignment reporter to write a story about the national budget.

"You know how complicated that is," Boccardi says. "Somebody sitting out there, trying to make some kind of sense of it? Have pity on the reader out there in Des Moines, trying to figure out what that means. If you send a reporter in there who doesn't understand the budget and the budget process, boy, it's tough to come out with a meaningful story. On the other hand, if there's a reporter who really knows, what a tremendous asset he can be."

To Boccardi, the challenge is encouraging beat reporters to use the sum of their knowledge in the stories they write—without veering off into opinion.

"The phrase I like to use is to 'report with authority.' . . . It means people who know their subject immensely well, whether you're talking about the statehouse in Austin or somebody on the space beat or somebody on Capitol Hill, there's a great deal of authority in the minds of our readers. And we need to ensure that that gets into the copy we write."

At the same time Boccardi knows that there will always be a need for general assignment reporters. The ideal, now and in the future, is a reporter with a literate liberal arts background along with some specialized expertise acquired in or out of school, he says.

"You know, one of the great things about being in this business . . . is you come to work every day not really knowing what you're going to do. You can be sent to interview a poet, you can be sent to a crime scene, you can be sent to cover a hostage situation at a bank or a speech by the treasury secretary on why a tax cut is needed and needed now.

"I'm not sure I can think of a specialized education that can equip you for those four things.

And that's not fanciful. That's the real world. I think one of the things that some people find interesting in journalists is that they can talk about anything for four minutes. And maybe that's not a bad asset."

9 Covering a Beat: The Courts

The Trial of Ennis Cosby's Killer

By **LINDA DEUTSCH**
AP Special Correspondent

SANTA MONICA, Calif. (AP)—A prosecutor opened her case against Mikail Markhasev today by seeking to prove through his own jailhouse writings that he is the killer of Ennis Cosby, pointing out that the defendant himself wrote it was "a robbery gone bad."

In her opening statement, Deputy District Attorney Anne Ingalls reconstructed for jurors the scene at the side of the road where Cosby was shot to death. And, with friends and family of Bill Cosby in the courtroom, she displayed graphic photos of the younger Cosby lying beside his car in a pool of blood.

Henry Hall, the lawyer for the defendant, said the case was a tragedy for both the Cosby and Markhasev families but insisted that police have charged the wrong man and that Markhasev is innocent.

By the end of the case, Hall said, "We will know who the killer is and it's not him."

Ingalls quoted Markhasev as using a racial epithet in allegedly confessing that he committed the killing and saying, "It's all over the news."

But Hall said that the racial epithet should not be part of the case.

"This case is not about racially charged issues, ethnicities or countries of origin, . . ." he said. "It is about whether my client, Mr. Markhasev, is the person who shot and killed Ennis Cosby. . . . This case is about a chance meeting. It's also a case full of mystery."

Cosby's only son, Ennis, 27, a graduate student at Columbia University, was fatally shot on Jan. 16, 1997, while changing a flat tire on a dark road.

Markhasev, 19, a Ukrainian immigrant with a history of gang affiliations and a previous brush with the law, was arrested nearly two months later.

The letter attributed by the prosecutor to Markhasev describes a plan to go to Bel-Air, a wealthy area of Los Angeles, and rob "a connection," apparently a drug dealer. But the letter says the target was not home.

The letter includes the statement: "The crime happened in Bel-Air. A robbery gone bad." It concludes: "I went to rob a connection and obviously found something else." It closes with a picture of a happy face and is signed "Peewee."

Ingalls called as her first witness police Detective John Garcia, who showed jurors enlargements of many letters allegedly written by Markhasev in jail to members of a Mexican prison gang.

The letters are filled with Spanish words and repeatedly refer to the recipients as "my homies."

The trial has gotten off to a speedy start. The jury of six men and six women was selected in less than two days last week, and Superior Court Judge David Perez has said he expects the panel to get the case by July 10.

Perez, 60, a 22-year veteran of the bench, has also decreed there will be no cameras in his courtroom because he does not want the trial to become a "TV episode."

"The absence of television cameras will lower the media temperature in this case," said UCLA Law School Professor Peter Arenella. "Without video footage to feed the magazine shows, it will not attract the same type of attention."

The nature of the case itself also is likely to tone down coverage, Arenella said.

"You don't have an interesting defendant, and the only celebrity involved is the father of the victim, who's doing his level best not to intrude on the proceedings," Arenella said. "It will be simple justice."

Bill Cosby was not expected at the trial.

During an appearance last weekend in Los Angeles, Cosby said "the family wants dignity" at the trial. Previously he and his wife, Camille, have said only that they want jurisprudence to take its course.

In an earlier court session, Ingalls described the case as "a gang case" and said many of her witnesses would come from the world of gangs and drug deals. The defense cited the possibility that the witnesses would have reasons to lie under oath.

"We're talking about people who had a motive to lay this crime off on Mikail Markhasev," said Hall. "We're not dealing with untainted people here."

Hall has promised to show that one of the key prosecution witnesses, Eli Zakaria, is more likely to be the killer than Markhasev.

By LINDA DEUTSCH
AP Special Correspondent

SANTA MONICA, Calif. (AP)—Prosecutors in the Ennis Cosby murder trial wrapped up their case with a strange twist, showing jurors a man the defense says is the real killer but without asking him any questions.

The abrupt finish came Friday after just five days of testimony.

Prosecutor Anne Ingalls had Los Angeles County sheriff's deputies march Eli Zakaria into the courtroom in handcuffs and a jail jumpsuit. It was a dramatic appearance by the man defense attorneys claim killed Bill Cosby's only son.

Zakaria said nothing but was told to stand only inches from the jury so the panelists could get a good look. He was then taken out of the courtroom.

"The people have no further witnesses," Ingalls announced without warning. Said Public Defender Henry Hall: "I'm obviously floored by the events of the last five minutes."

The defense told jurors in opening statements that Zakaria is the person depicted in a composite drawing of the killer. The prosecution claims the drawing is a match for Mikail Markhasev, the 19-year-old Ukrainian immigrant who is on trial.

The prosecution had listed Zakaria and his girlfriend, Sara Peters, on the witness list but never called them to testify. Police have said Zakaria and Peters were in a car with Markhasev the night Cosby was shot to death.

Laurie Levenson, dean of the Loyola University law school, said the prosecutor's move was a surprise.

"If they said they had a mountain of evidence in the O. J. Simpson trial, this is a molehill," she said. "It's a lot thinner than what people expect in a high-profile case."

Hall said he was not ready to present defense witnesses on Monday. The judge gave him until Wednesday, after hearings on who may testify.

Moments before she brought Zakaria into court, Ingalls called a detective who played an obscenity-laced tape of Markhasev and friend Michael Chang in which Chang, cooperating with police, tried to get Markhasev to make incriminating statements.

"They're talking about the Cosby thing," Chang said at one point, complaining that he is being harassed by police.

"I don't know anything about no Cosby thing," Markhasev says. "I don't know what the (obscenity) you're talking about. What's Cosby got to do with this?"

On the tape, Markhasev hints he is fearful the conversation is being recorded, telling Chang, "What's wrong with you, you're talking from a work phone."

Chang had suggested he was calling from his job although he was actually sitting in the Los Angeles Police Department's robbery-homicide division.

The conversation ends with Markhasev suggesting Chang should come and see him in person at his home because they needed to talk.

"You didn't do anything wrong," Markhasev said. "What are you worried about? I didn't do anything wrong either. Everything's cool."

LAPD Detective Michael Bercham testified about how the tape was made. He said Markhasev was under surveillance and surrounded on March 12, 1997, at his home.

Chang, who was held in contempt for refusing to testify, was present when Markhasev admitted shooting a black man and helped him in an unsuccessful search for a gun, according to another witness, Christopher So.

A police search later located a gun wrapped in a knit cap, which police witnesses said contained a single hair that had DNA matching Markhasev's.

Cosby, 27, was shot as he changed a flat tire along a dark road on Jan. 16, 1997. The prosecutor has said Markhasev is a member of the Mexican mafia prison gang.

So was the only witness to say Markhasev admitted shooting a black man, and he described Markhasev frantically searching for a gun about five miles from the killing scene days later.

But So has also told jurors that a tabloid newspaper paid him $40,000 for interviews and promised him a $100,000 reward if it led to a conviction. He acknowledged becoming involved in the case only after The National Enquirer announced a reward and said he never went to police with his claims.

Police came to him after his contact with the Enquirer. Markhasev's defense suggested that So, a convicted embezzler, was less than forthright.

Levenson said the key evidence is a series of incriminating jailhouse letters said to be written by Markhasev, the tiny hair tied to Markhasev through DNA analysis, So's testimony and the audio tape.

"This is Markhasev vs. Markhasev," she said. "If he had kept his mouth shut and his pen down he wouldn't be sitting in the courtroom."

By LINDA DEUTSCH
AP Special Correspondent

SANTA MONICA, Calif. (AP)—A young man with a history of gang affiliations was found guilty Tuesday in the slaying of Bill Cosby's only son, Ennis, as he changed a flat tire on a dark and lonely road last year.

Several members of the Cosby family, including two of the victim's sisters, Erika and Erinn, wept and hugged as the verdicts were read. The entertainer and his wife were not in the courtroom.

Mikail Markhasev, a 19-year-old Ukrainian immigrant, also was convicted of attempting to rob Cosby and using a firearm in the commission of attempted robbery.

The jury's finding on all counts automatically mandates a life prison term with no possibility of parole. Formal sentencing was scheduled for Aug. 11.

"The Cosby family is satisfied with the judicial process that has led to this conviction," Cosby spokesman David Brokaw said. "They have no comment on the sentencing."

Prosecutors had opted not to seek the death penalty, but did not give a reason. The defendant's age was believed to be a major consideration.

Included in the family group in court was Phil Caputo, the man who played basketball with Ennis Cosby hours before he was killed. Caputo had tears in his eyes as he heard the word "guilty."

The family of Markhasev never made it to the courtroom in time to hear the verdicts. Markhasev stood stonefaced, staring at the jury as the verdicts were read.

Defense attorney Henry Hall said of his client's reaction to the life sentence: "He's 19 years old and it doesn't take a rocket scientist to figure out how he feels about that," Hall said.

He blamed the media rather than the celebrity of the Cosby family for the conviction.

Cosby, 27, a vacationing graduate student from Columbia University, was fatally shot Jan. 16, 1997, while changing a flat tire on a dark road near Bel-Air. Markhasev was arrested nearly two months later.

The victim was a child of privilege who overcame the adversity of learning problems and was on the brink of receiving his master's degree in special education.

His father, eloquent in his grief, summed up his loss simply after the shooting: "He was my hero."

Cosby was shot on his way to meet a new acquaintance, Stephanie Crane, who would testify that Cosby called and said he had a flat. She offered to help, drove to his location and used her car's headlights to illuminate his mother's Mercedes-Benz while he changed the tire.

Nearby, three people had stopped their car near a public telephone, the prosecutor said; one of them was Markhasev, who had served time in a juvenile correctional facility.

Crane remembered only that she was sitting in her Jaguar when a young man approached.

"All of a sudden a man's face appeared in my window," she testified. "He said, 'Open your door or I'll shoot.'"

The witness said she pulled forward, thinking that if she shined her car's lights on the man he would be scared away.

"When I turned around I couldn't see Ennis. I started screaming, 'Ennis! Ennis!' . . . Then I saw this person in the distance running. I looked down and I saw Ennis on the ground."

Who was the man who ran away? Crane couldn't tell. She failed to pick Markhasev out of a police lineup.

Crane was the prosecution's only eyewitness.

The jury, which heard testimony over two weeks, spent less than six hours talking over the case before accepting the prosecution's argument that Markhasev had been convicted by his own words.

"The whole thing was open and shut, or at least close to that. The evidence was there loud and clear," said juror Joseph Burnett Vagner, 78.

Prosecutor Anne Ingalls had used a series of jailhouse letters she said were written by the defendant and a profanity-laced recorded phone conversation in which Markhasev sounded frantic and concerned that a friend was mentioning Cosby's name.

The prosecution also relied on a single tiny hair linked to the defendant by DNA testing. The hair was found in a knit cap wrapped around the gun identified as the murder weapon.

Ingalls had unsuccessfully lobbied the judge to keep jurors' names secret in the case, saying the defendant was a "made" member of the Mexican mafia and that jurors could be subject to retaliation. A "made" member is one who is formally initiated into a gang.

The defense claimed that police arrested the wrong man, that the letters were forged and the phone conversation was the prattling of a teen-ager discussing a dope deal.

The case went to the jury Monday after Bill Cosby made his first court appearance on the last day of arguments. He had stayed away from the trial until then, saying he wanted to preserve the dignity of the proceeding.

Defense attorneys attacked the testimony of informant Christopher So, who led police to where the gun was found and said he heard Markhasev tell another friend: "I shot a nigger. It's all over the news. It's big."

The defense attorneys said jurors should not accept the word of a convicted felon who sold his story to the National Enquirer.

Ingalls had said that Markhasev essentially convicted himself with letters he wrote in jail referring to details of the crime.

"The letters are everything in this case," Ingalls said, and went on to read statements such as: "It was a robbery gone bad."

Outside the courthouse, District Attorney Gill Garcetti said: "We are pleased that justice was done in this case, we are pleased for the Cosby family."

Until 1994 Linda Deutsch was able to ply her trade quietly. She covered trials—big trials, some of the biggest in American history—and though her byline was common in newspapers around the world, few of those who read her stories about the Manson trial or the Exxon Valdez trial or the Rodney King trial would recognize her face.

But then O. J. Simpson was charged with murder, and everything changed.

Early on, during jury selection, Deutsch was the only reporter allowed in the courtroom, serving as the pool reporter for all the rest, and Americans grew accustomed to turning on their televisions and seeing this wire-service reporter—traditionally, the most anonymous of species—read her notes. She became a sort of celebrity. The Los Angeles Times complained. "The responsibility this places on the shoulders of even a reporter of Linda Deutsch's high caliber is daunting," it said.

By the time the trial began, she had reverted to her more traditional role. Once again Deutsch was the dean of the press section. Editors across the country looked to her stories each day to explain what on earth was happening in that circus in Los Angeles.

Once a television reporter ran up to Deutsch and disagreed with the lead she had written for that day's story. "You're setting the agenda for the entire country!" the reporter cried.

"I looked at her, and I said, 'No, I'm just reporting the story.' You have to keep your own focus very clearly and not be dissuaded by the opinions of others," Deutsch says.

As Deutsch will tell you, scoops are not common in the courts: "Everybody is in there seeing the same story at the same time. The only difference is interpretation and presentation. And how you see it."

A New Jersey girl, she came to California in the 1960s. She was hired by the AP in Los Angeles in 1967; she wanted to write about entertainment, and she enjoyed interviewing stars, reviewing movies, covering the Oscars. But as a new reporter, she did what all new reporters do at the AP: She worked weekends, filed the broadcast wire.

Then, five minutes after she arrived at work one night in June

1968, Robert F. Kennedy was killed in the Ambassador Hotel in Los Angeles. She worked for two days straight. When Kennedy's assassin, Sirhan Sirhan, went on trial, the AP sent reporters from Washington and New York to cover the story; Deutsch was assigned to help out—to write the sidebars, to do the minor stuff.

A year later she was out at the airport to report on the arrival of President Richard Nixon, who was flying in to see his San Clemente home for the first time, when she heard from her office. "Forget Nixon," her editor said. "There's this big story breaking."

The "big story" was the gruesome discovery of the bloody bodies of actress Sharon Tate and four other people in a house in Benedict Canyon. The next night two more bodies were found across town. Three months would pass before the authorities arrested Charles Manson and his murderous family.

The AP sent legendary trial reporter Arthur Everett to cover the trial. He would write the story for the morning papers, and Deutsch—by now considered an apprentice trial reporter—would write it for the afternoon papers.

"But there was one problem," she says. "Art came out, and he took one look at this scene—which included the defendants jumping up and down screaming, being dragged out of the courtroom, people having LSD flashbacks in the courtroom, people being arrested for trying to smuggle heroin in, the Manson girls camped on the sidewalk outside, carving X's in their heads and saying they're going to immolate themselves. And there were estimates that the trial would last a year. After a short time, a couple of weeks, I think, Art—who was such a gentle soul, dignified, always dignified, always had a handkerchief in his pocket—came up to me and said, 'You know, I think I have a vacation scheduled.'

"And he left and never came back. And for the balance of the 10½ months of the Manson trial I covered it alone. Talk about a trial by fire. . . . After that I was considered a trial expert."

She became a member of a roving group of trial reporters who wandered from one big trial to another. She did not miss entertainment writing: "By that point I had found that the real-life courtroom drama was much more exciting than anything I would ever encounter on the great silver screen or behind it, and it had become very entrancing. . . . It was very life-altering."

It also has been, at times, a challenge. She is not a lawyer, and despite more than 30 years covering trials, she occasionally encounters legalisms she does not understand.

"Lawyers love to talk. It's just a basic," she says. "And they love to talk mostly about their business. If you are confused about anything, or you don't understand it, or you have a very technical legal term that comes up in court and you think, 'What the heck is that?' ask a lawyer. They will almost always take the time to answer you. Even if there's a gag order in a case, which is my pet peeve, a lawyer is not prevented from answering you to explain the law."

Her favorite example is the case of the Exxon Valdez, which spilled 11 million gallons of oil in Alaska's Prince William Sound. Not only was she exported from warm and sunny Southern California to Alaska in January. (Her bureau chief told his superiors, "Well, yes, Deutsch is available, but Deutsch doesn't have clothes for Alaska." And so, she recalls, "they had to get me long underwear and a parka and boots and all that stuff.") She also discovered upon her arrival that "the entire thing was based on maritime law, which was something I had never even heard of. The law of the seas. And I thought, 'What they heck am I going to do?' I went up to one of the lawyers who was representing Captain (Joseph) Hazlewood, and I said, 'Can you tell me about maritime law?' And he said, 'That's my specialty. That's all I do, and I'll be glad to tell you anything you need to know.'"

Lawyers are her best sources of information. "Clerks are good for keeping track of what's going on. Beyond that, they usually don't know more than what a lawyer knows. They'll know a lot about the judge, and if they'll talk to you, they'll tell you if he's inclined to postpone something. They're not going to tell you anything too inside because their own careers could be jeopardized."

She also makes it her business to get to know judges whenever possible. Because the judges control the courtroom. "Without access, you're dead. You have to be able to have access to the courtroom, access to the records, to the documents in the case. And the judge controls all of that," she says.

She is always ready to call an AP lawyer if a judge tries to close his or her courtroom to reporters: "If you cover the courts, you have to be a fighter for the First Amendment. You have to defend your right to be there."

Before the start of the trial of Mikail Markhasev, Deutsch gathered representatives of the press corps to meet with Superior Court Judge David Perez to hash out access issues. He agreed to give the news media adequate seating. He was thinking of empaneling an anonymous jury, "which would have been terrible for us," Deutsch says. "Not because I want their names. I don't. For my audience, they could care less what the names are. But I want to know whether this is a welder from Gardena or if it's a lawyer from Beverly Hills. I need to know some details about these people."

She is, she says, "a jury-selection nut. Nobody can believe it, but I like to sit through every minute of jury selection. Because if you're really trying to gauge what the lawyers are doing and how they are structuring their cases, you have to know who is sitting in that box. Because they know. It also turns out to be a social study if you're interested in the jury system and how it works and who's participating in it."

Ultimately, the judge in the Cosby case agreed to ask each prospective juror if he or she had any objection to personal information being made public. Of the 300 people interviewed, only one objected.

The time before the trial was given over to preparation. As Deutsch explains, "Preparing for trials is different for every one. Because the characters are different, the issues are different. . . . But there are certain nuts-and-bolts things. You talk to the prosecutors. Get the documentation and find out what it's all about. If there are witnesses that you know . . . try to find out about them. I'm not big on pre-trial interviews of witnesses, because you risk prejudicing the trial. . . .

"Basically, it's knowing everything about the crime and where it happened, when it happened. All of that is going to come up in testimony, and so I try to make a list in advance, sometimes carry a little notebook that has all the facts."

She met the prosecutor and Markhasev's public defender. She knows that reporters are not popular with the peculiar community that assembles to conduct a trial: "I think you have to realize that when you walk into a big trial, nobody wants you there. You are not invited. The defendant would rather not have his picture in the paper and his story in the paper, the defense lawyers would rather try their case quietly, the prosecutors think you're going to impede their effort to convict, and the judge thinks he's going to be seen as a fool. Other than that . . . You have to win friends and influence people from the get-go."

She checked on when documents were being filed, including the trial memorandum, which outlines the case: "The documents often produce the best stories."

When the trial began, she took her customary seat on the aisle in the front row: "That's my seat. Because I want to get out in a hurry if necessary. I don't want to climb over people."

She listened to the opening statements, "road maps for the trial. You also want to keep a record of them because sometimes they'll promise something and they won't deliver."

The Cosby trial, with one exception, offered few big surprises. This was a robbery gone wrong. "It involved a celebrity son, it involved drugs, there was some bizarre testimony about the drug house where these people lived, and it gave an insight into what was going on on the fringes of Hollywood, Bel-Air, wherever they were living. There were drugs, there was money, there were all the things that make for cases that intrigue the public," Deutsch says.

The one surprise was the moment when the prosecutors called a witness, brought him into the courtroom, and then did not ask him a question.

"Pretty weird. Pretty tense. We had no idea that she would bring this guy in and not let him speak a word. We thought that he would be a witness. This was somebody they suspected was the real killer. The public defender claimed that," she explains. The prosecution wanted to show that the witness, Eli Zakaria, did not match the description of Ennis Cosby's killer. But the prosecutors knew that if they asked him about the murder, he would refuse to answer under the Fifth Amendment's guarantee against self-incrimination. If he did that, jurors might be convinced that he was the murderer. So they asked him nothing.

Most days Deutsch would fill an entire notebook. She writes everything down because she'd rather have too much than too little. She does not use shorthand; she just writes fast, writing both the lawyers' questions and the witnesses' answers, stinting when she has to on the questions. Other reporters often check with her for the exact wording of quotes; from time to time she has checked her notes against the official trial transcripts: "The only thing I'm ever missing is a 'the' or maybe an 'and.' "

"If it's a particularly crucial set of quotes, everybody wants to be on the same page. So we check with each other, unless we're on deadline and I'm dictating."

In fact, she prefers to dictate rather than writing her stories on a computer: "It's faster. I'm able to organize my thoughts very quickly as to what was very important, what struck me at that moment. And I don't have to run to a computer." With cellular phones, the days when she had to run to a pay phone to dictate—and sometimes fight with another reporter for that phone—are just unpleasant memories.

A key to her dictation is her system of note taking. As she goes along, she underlines in red everything that is crucial to the story. "If I see the lead coming at me, I put a big red star on it. Once I walk out of the courtroom, I know what the lead is, usually. And then it's just backing it up."

A few years ago, when the Society for Professional Journalists roasted her, someone produced a video in which young reporters were instructed on how to cover a trial the way Linda Deutsch does. You have to bring two pens to court, they were told, one black and one red. And you have to underline what is important. They held up a big pad, and what was underlined was "GUILTY GUILTY GUILTY."

The Cosby trial lasted weeks; Bill Cosby attended the closing arguments. The jury deliberated for just six hours, and Deutsch dictated the verdict on her cell phone.

"The verdict itself is such an emotional moment in any case," she says. "For the people involved—for the witnesses, the victims, and of course the defendant, all their families—this may be the most important moment in their lives."

She has seen younger reporters—and some veteran writers—who were so stunned by the impact of the moment that they stopped taking notes: "They will sit there with their mouths open."

But not Linda Deutsch. She keeps writing.

10 Covering a Beat: Science and Medicine

Using Radiation to Fix a Heart

By DANIEL Q. HANEY
AP Medical Editor

BOSTON (AP)—The first hour of the angioplasty went normally, assuming of course that shoving wires, balloons, drills and other gadgetry into the heart of a wide-awake man can ever be considered normal. But then something out of the ordinary happened.

Dr. Daniel Simon leaned toward his patient, who was covered neck to toe in sterile blue cloth. Even with his glasses on, the patient could see nothing but a big X-ray camera hanging overhead. Out of view were 10 doctors, nurses and technicians, all wearing knee-length lead vests and waiting for this moment.

"Mark, we've got the artery wide open," Simon said in a reassuring voice. "Now we are going to irradiate."

Radiation in the form of X-rays has long been used during heart procedures to take pictures of the work in progress. But this was different. The doctors were about to try to fix a bad heart using the same kind of radiation usually reserved for killing cancer.

Such a seemingly extreme approach was necessary, at least in part, because the other technology in the small, crowded room had already made this bad heart even worse. Except for his young age—38—the patient was a typical failure of modern cardiology.

What first brought him here was angina, the pain that seized his chest whenever he did anything demanding, like ride a bike. The problem was his heart's right coronary artery. Last winter, doctors discovered it was two-thirds plugged. So his heart's own muscle was starved of oxygen-carrying blood. At the time, the solution seemed obvious: He needed an angioplasty.

In 23 years, this procedure has grown to be one of the most common big-ticket treatments in medicine, now done about 750,000 times a year in the United States.

Common, but hardly foolproof, and certainly not for Mark. He became one of the unfortunate, sizable minority whose angioplasties go bad.

Within a few weeks, the pain was back, worse than before. Now his chest hurt even when he did nothing. The reopened artery had clogged with a vengeance. The medical word for this is "restenosis," and in Mark's case, it meant the flow of blood was 99 percent blocked.

Doctors repeated the procedure, but the result was the same. So now, five months and two angioplasties later, Mark was back in the cardiac catheterization lab, two stories below ground at Brigham and Women's Hospital, ready for something new.

The doctors began the job by threading a delivery tube from his groin up into his heart. First, they sent in a tiny diamond-tipped conical burr. Spinning at 180,000 rpm, it chewed through the gunk that clogged his artery. Next they inserted a skinny sausage-shaped balloon. When briefly inflated, it squeezed the artery a little wider, leaving a reasonably normal three-millimeter opening.

Now came something called the Beta-Cath system. This rig is a gun the size of an electric drill that uses hydraulic pressure to drive seeds of radioactive strontium 90 through a catheter into the heart. Simon maneuvered the catheter into Mark's bad artery.

A radiation oncologist—the only specialist licensed to deliver this powerful stuff—held the gun and pushed the switch, sending in the seeds. A technician counted down the seconds, "30 . . . 29 . . . 28 . . ." In half a minute, the seeds returned to the gun, and it was over.

Around the world, perhaps 6,000 heart patients have been treated with radiation this way, most of them—like the Boston patient—in formal research studies. However, radiation could be routinely available within a year. Novoste Corp. of Norcross, Ga. recently asked the Food and Drug Administration for approval to sell its Beta-Cath. Competing systems are being developed by Guidant Corp. of Indianapolis and Johnson & Johnson's Cordis unit, among others.

Radiation has long been viewed as the heaviest of medical artillery. That cardiologists would even consider using it against their old nemesis, restenosis, shows just how close to wits' end they have come.

This is the latest in a succession of medical technologies intended to prevent or correct what happened to Mark. Most were used enthusiastically for a year or two, then abandoned when they proved no better, and sometimes worse, than plain balloon angioplasty.

"For the longest time, restenosis has been the Achilles' heel of interventional cardiology," says Dr. Tony Farah of Allegheny General Hospital in Pittsburgh.

From the very start, actually. Dr. Andreas R. Gruentzig did the first balloon angioplasty in 1977 in Zurich with equipment he designed in his kitchen. Soon it became apparent that reopened heart arteries often closed off again within six months or so.

Nevertheless, angioplasty took off. Its power to make people feel better instantly—and get out of the hospital in just a day—made it an attractive alternative to the rigors of coronary bypass surgery.

But it was always a gamble. After one-third to one-half of seemingly successful angioplasties, the artery clogs up again. In half the cases where this happens, the renarrowing is so severe that patients need another procedure—either a repeat angioplasty or a bypass operation.

Over the years, engineers tinkered with many clever but ultimately ineffective solutions. Whirring knives carved the buildup away; lasers burned it off. While the diamond-tipped burr and a few other methods are still used occasionally, none does much in the long run to prevent restenosis.

Until now, the only thing to make any difference is something called a stent. These elegantly designed stainless steel mesh tubes are the one true breakthrough of the first two decades of angioplasty.

Cardiologists push the folded-up stents into place after an angioplasty balloon squeezes open the artery. There the stents spring open and lock, acting as stiff metal scaffolds to prop the artery open.

This prevents the most common cause of failure after ordinary balloon angioplasty, which is artery recoil. The artery wall is springy like a rubber tube, and without a stent it often just returns to its original shape when the balloon is gone.

Studies show stents reduce angioplasty failure by about 40 percent, but many experts doubt they are truly that effective. Almost nothing in medicine works as well in everyday practice as it does in formal studies, where patients tend to be healthier and better cared for.

Nevertheless, more than 80 percent of patients get stents during their angioplasties, despite questions about whether this is necessary.

Dr David Brown of Montefiore Medical Center in New York City reviewed more than 44,000 angioplasties done in California in 1997. His conclusion: About 20 percent of all patients eventually needed a bypass operation or repeat angioplasty, regardless of whether or not they got stents.

However, preventing restenosis is not the only reason for stents' popularity.

The biggest health risk after an angioplasty is the abrupt total blockage of the artery, something that can happen in the first few days after the procedure. It occurs when a flap of artery wall is torn loose during the angioplasty and drops down to plug the flow. Unlike garden-variety restenosis, this is a life-threatening crisis. It complicates 3 percent to 5 percent of angioplasties and usually requires emergency bypass for repair.

Stents plaster back these tears so they cannot trigger disaster. "Stents have almost eliminated the need for emergency bypass surgery as a complication of angioplasty," says Dr. Larry S. Dean of the University of Alabama in Birmingham.

But stents also create a new problem—a particularly intractable variety of restenosis, the very thing they were designed to prevent. Stents spur the growth of scar tissue over the damage left by the balloon. These cells can quickly grow through the stent's steel mesh, sometimes entirely filling the artery.

This turns out to be a problem for perhaps 15 percent to 20 percent of stent patients, and it is hard to fix. Doctors can ream out the plugged stent with burrs and balloons, but the artery usually fills up again.

The need to control renarrowing worsened by stents explains doctors' willingness to experiment with radiation. The idea is to kill the rapidly dividing cells that form scar tissue. Without this growth, the thinking goes, stent-braced arteries will keep flowing.

The first U.S. doctor to try this was Paul Teirstein of the Scripps Clinic in San Diego. His first patient happened to be a fellow physician who had endured five failed angioplasties in 10 months. The man pleaded for something new. Teirstein mentioned experiments in rabbits and pigs showing that radiation might prevent recurring blockage.

" 'If it works in pigs, it will probably work in me,' " Teirstein remembers the man saying. "We irradiated him, and it worked. He didn't have any more restenosis."

That was 1994, and it began the development of the competing radiation approaches that are nearing Food and Drug Administration approval.

The technologies differ somewhat. Some, such as the Beta-Cath, use beta radiation that penetrates only a few millimeters into the artery, so doctors and nurses can stay in the room without getting hit by it. Other systems use farther-reaching gamma radiation, so everyone but the patient must leave the room while the artery is being zapped.

While the various techniques have not been compared head to head, they seem roughly equal, reducing the return of restenosis by between one-third and one-half.

Whether radiation will work this well for Mark remains to be seen, since the regrowth that blocks stents can take several weeks.

From what they have seen so far, many doctors are convinced radiation will be a routine part of heart treatment, at least until something better comes along.

There is a deceptive quality to Dan Haney's work; he takes the most complicated medical stories and makes them understandable to readers who wouldn't know the difference between a stent and a stunt. Part of it is sheer longevity; he has covered medicine for decades and has developed a real understanding of the healing arts. But mostly Haney works hard to make it look simple. And he uses both imagination and common sense to make stories come alive.

That is how he ended up in an operating room, watching surgeons irradiate a man's blood vessels. But perhaps it would be better to let Haney tell his own story:

I write more about heart disease than any other medical problem. That's because it is the leading cause of death and is something that almost everybody gets, in some form, even if it's not what ultimately kills a person. It's just plain newsworthy. It's also, in an odd way, a fun subject to write about. It interests me. That's because, unlike cancer, there is a lot of real progress. There is always something new to say. In the 20-odd years I've been covering medicine, many new kinds of drugs have become routine, such as the cholesterol-lowering statins. The world has learned about all the habits that contribute to heart disease, such as bad diets and sloth. And tons of new technological gadgetry has come into play. These have been great spot stories, and there are always opportunities to put the piecemeal and often conflicting individual results into perspective.

We tend to write about each of these new pieces of hardware on its own, usually with great enthusiasm at the start, and then simply let them drop if they fail to hold up. But over the years I've become increasingly interested in how all these advances fit together. (For instance, I did a story a couple of years ago about how all the glowingly reported treatments that keep damaged hearts beating have led to a vast increase in the number of people suffering from congestive heart failure. In an earlier time they would have died from their heart disease before they got this awful condition.)

For several years I have thought about doing a story about the complications of angioplasty. In particular, I'm intrigued by the common failure of an angioplasty to hold up over time. (The artery closes up again. Docs call this restenosis.) I've heard many presentations on various ingenious devices intended to solve the problem, but almost all of them have been abandoned because they don't in the end prevent restenosis. The story I wrote is really about this arms race, all the attempts to overcome a central shortcoming of angioplasty that has bedeviled the procedure from the very start.

My story ideas come from several places. Number one is medical meetings. I attend 10 or 12 a year. This is where the latest ideas and the controversies and uncertainties about medical practice get discussed. Number two is medical journals. And a very, very distant number three is press releases and pitches from PR people.

The first time I heard of radiation for restenosis was at a meeting of the American Heart Association in New Orleans in 1966. Dr. Paul Teirstein from the Scripps Clinic, who pioneered this approach, gave a presentation on about 50 patients. It seemed to

work well. But obviously it was early in the game and too soon to know if it would pan out. At that time Dr. Spencer King from Emory, one of the country's best-known cardiologists, said he was working on a competing technology (the predecessor of the Beta-Cath in my story), and he called the results "amazing." I wrote up a 600-word spot story and promptly forgot about it.

Then, at an American College of Cardiology meeting in Anaheim, I attended a briefing for medical writers about advances in various areas of cardiology. Dr. John Hirshfeld of the University of Pennsylvania walked us through all the different, mostly failed technologies, and at the end he spoke skeptically about radiation: "We're talking about a pretty heavy-duty intervention to deliver radiation to people who don't have cancer or other diseases that will shorten their lives considerably."

It occurred to me then that this could be an interesting intro into the whole business of angioplasty failure. The meeting was huge, about 30,000 people, and I kept looking for feature leads while writing spot stories. Dozens of public relations people pitched story ideas, mostly garbage. But near the end of the meeting, one PR guy who actually had given me some useful things in the past handed me a fat folder of information about one of his clients and pleaded with me to at least look at it. The company turned out to be one that makes a radiation delivery device for heart patients.

After pitching the idea to my editor, I began by reading up on the subject. I wanted to find out more about the specifics of radiation during angioplasty as well as the history of earlier attempts to prevent restenosis. Much of the information on earlier devices I got from reading my own stories from the AP archive as well as by visiting some Web sites devoted to angioplasty. Some of the technical detail about the radiation came from the three manufacturers' Web pages and press kits. Another good source was medical journal articles, most of which I found on the Web.

However, the single most important source of information was doctor interviews. I attempted to find cardiologists who both are experts on angioplasty and its shortcomings and

know something about the radiation devices, which still have not been approved by the FDA. That meant they probably had been involved in the company-sponsored studies of the devices or at least were medical school docs who kept up with the latest research.

I put out a query on Profnet. I got a couple of dozen responses. Using those and other names I ran across from my reading and experience, I made up a list of 18 people I wanted to talk to. I eventually spoke to most of them. (I like to interview a lot of people for stories, even though most of them never make it into the final product. That is the only way I can gauge the consensus opinion on complicated subjects. With all of this background, I feel I can write authoritatively without having to bog the story down with unnecessary attribution of widely accepted facts.)

I did quite a lot of background reading before I ever called anyone. Docs can be skittish interviewees. Their biggest fear is that they will be made to look foolish in front of their colleagues. Therefore, they sometimes get very antsy if they perceive that you are ill informed and might get the story wrong. When interviewing docs, it helps if you can use their language. Cardiologists feel comfortable with words like "infarction," "ischemia" and "perfusion," and it reassures them if you understand these words and use them yourself. The only problem with this is that you risk getting technobabble quotes that are unusable in a story. (One way to overcome this is to ask simple, what's-it-all-mean questions at the end of the interview, when you know the plain English quotes you're looking for.)

I did most of my interviews on the phone. I type like a machine gun and can get almost a full transcript of the conversation. Some of my interview notes are over 2,000 words long.

Often in reporting about medicine, there is not much to see. That's especially true of drug development. But I like to get to the scene of the action when possible, because the specific details can make a story much more readable. In this case I thought it would be interesting to actually watch the radiation being delivered. I knew that Brigham and Women's Hospital in Boston was one of the places that used the radiation experimentally. So I asked its PR department to help arrange for me to watch a procedure.

The last time I did something like that had been a year earlier, when I had written a feature about using gene therapy to reverse otherwise untreatable heart disease. I wanted to see the genes actually being injected into the heart. I witnessed that operation at St. Elizabeth's Hospital in Boston. I remember how bloodless and somehow detached the process seemed to be. The surgeon deftly opened up the man's chest, exposed his heart, and injected DNA into it. That provided what seemed, to me, to be fascinating color that brought an otherwise abstract idea to life. Here's how I began that story:

> " 'Genes,' ordered the surgeon. Then he injected a syringe of pure DNA and salt water into a man's beating yellow-red heart. Dr. James Symes stared for a moment into his patient's chest. The incision began just below the left nipple, ran through the lumpy layers of fat and muscle, then between the ribs, finally exposing the heart. The surgeon moved the needle an inch. Again he slid it into the pulsing surface. And again. And again."

I hoped that lead would draw the readers into the story and make them want to read about the rather dense and forbidding subject of gene therapy. It occurred to me that the radiation treatment might also offer interesting color, although I did not know if it would be compelling enough to lead the story with.

That morning of the radiation procedure, it was raining. I met the AP photographer in the lobby of the big teaching hospital, and a PR guy escorted us through a maze of corridors two stories belowground to the room where the procedure would be done. I had never seen an angioplasty, although I knew basically what to expect from having written about it so much. We changed into surgical scrubs and were told to put on heavy lead vests. This was perhaps the biggest surprise of the morning. The things weigh a ton. It was exhausting to stand around in them. The vests weren't just for the radiation procedure. Docs and nurses wear these things for all angioplasties, since X-rays are needed to take images.

The room where the procedure was done is called a cath (short for catheterization) lab. It's not an operating room, and this is not surgery. It's considered a procedure. The room was surprisingly small and was filled with nine or 10 doctors, technicians and nurses. The cardiologist, a young, friendly, confidence-inspiring man named Daniel Simon, was already at work, getting the catheter in place to do the procedure, which would involve an angioplasty, a Roto-Rooter affair and the radiation. Occasionally Simon told me what was going on. But mostly he concentrated on the angioplasty, which appeared to be technologically quite complicated.

I stood out of his way and scribbled in a notebook. I wrote down things like the speed of the Roto-Rooter, the size of the wire stent used to prop open the artery and the width of the patient's reopened artery. I made notes on the colors in the room, the sounds, the monitoring machines, the occasional, sparse conversation among the medical team. I gathered in all the technical detail I could see. I had no idea how much of this I would eventually use. I might have asked a question or two, but I pretty much kept my mouth shut. I felt privileged to be there but an intruder too, and I didn't want to in any way mess up the procedure.

By the time it was over, I had taken 21 pages of notes. Outside the cath lab, Simon sat down at a machine used to read angiograms— X-ray movies of the heart arteries— and showed me what he had done.

It's hard to say exactly how much time I put into the story, since my day is constantly interrupted with calls from bureaus, editing desks and public relations people. But I worked at it on and off for about three weeks. The doctor interviews are especially hard to arrange. The docs are usually eager to talk, but they have killer schedules, and it can take a week for them to find a spare half-hour for an interview.

Organizing the material was a challenge. I usually try to avoid starting stories with anecdotes. I think this approach is hackneyed and often a fallback when people can't think of a way to summarize their reporting. In this case, though, I thought the anecdote nicely encapsulated all the issues I intended to write about. The patient was both a beneficiary and a victim of modern cardiology.

The story was really about the persistent failure of angioplasty and all the technological attempts to make it more reliable. By starting with this case, I had a framework for discussing all these tools, including the newest one, as well as the stent; I think most people have heard of stents, but they really have been a mixed blessing for patients.

I went through my thousands of words of interviews and picked out the best quotes and copied them onto a separate page. I also took note of all the major points raised in the interviews and listed them on another sheet. Finally, I made a list of all the points I wanted to cover in the story.

The writing itself took the better part of a week, given the constant interruptions. And when it was done—when the story found its way into newspapers around the country—I moved on to something else.

Just as doctors never lack for patients or illnesses to treat, medical writers never have to scrounge for stories about new health hazards or advances in medicine.

11 Covering a Beat: Television

Who Wants to Insure a "Millionaire" Show?

By DAVID BAUDER
AP Television Writer

NEW YORK (AP)—The company that insures ABC's hit game show, "Who Wants to Be a Millionaire," is suing to get out of its contract because it claims the questions are too easy and they're at risk of paying out too much prize money.

ABC says viewers shouldn't worry about the legal fight—they're planning no changes to the show.

The London-based insurance underwriters Goshawk Syndicate filed suit in Britain's High Court of Justice on Jan. 24 against Buena Vista Entertainment, Inc., the show's producers, to end its contract.

In essence, Goshawk said it needed assurances that "Who Wants to Be a Millionaire" would ask harder questions and select dumber contestants.

"Millionaire" has been the television sensation of the year, frequently pulling in 30 million viewers a night and pro-pelling ABC to the top of the ratings. Host Regis Philbin's question—"Is that your final answer?"—has become a national catchphrase.

Other television networks have quickly tried to imitate "Millionaire," to mixed success.

Under its contract, Goshawk is required to pay out prize money to contestants who win $500,000 or more on the show. There's a deductible of $1.5 million before Goshawk is required to pay and a ceiling of $5 million. That means, for example, Goshawk would only be required to pay prizes to five winners of $1 million.

Reached in London on Thursday, a spokeswoman for Goshawk refused to comment.

"Unquestionably, the integrity of the show is above reproach and nobody is claiming otherwise," ABC spokeswoman Julie Hoover said. "This is simply a dispute in which the company providing insurance is trying to get out of coverage on the basis of a conversation it had with a broker."

Two "Millionaire" contestants—an Internal Revenue Service agent from Connecticut and a Miami attorney—correctly answered 15 questions and won $1 million. By contrast, no player on the original British version of the game show has ever won the big prize.

Through 51 shows, there have also been three $500,000 winners. "Millionaire" has given out a total of $9,314,000 in prize money since it has been on the air, according to ABC.

The multiple-choice questions are frequently easy in the early rounds. One contestant was asked which condiment is also known as a Latin dance, correctly choosing salsa over the other options: mustard, mayonnaise and relish.

They get harder as the stakes grow higher. The first million-dollar winner won by correctly identifying the U.S. president to appear on the television show "Laugh-In" (Richard Nixon). The second had to know the distance between the Earth and the sun (93 million miles).

Simply getting on the show can actually be harder than winning big money: it requires potential contestants to successfully navigate a three-tier elimination process where they are judged on speed and accuracy.

In the lawsuit, Goshawk said it needed "significant changes in the level of control" to "reduce the unacceptable level of losses." Specifically, the syndicate asked for changes in the method of contestant selection and the degree of difficulty of the questions.

Since no changes were made since it first asked for them in late December, Goshawk said that "substantial losses under the insurance are expected."

Hoover was not sure what the next step in the case would be.

Even if the show's producers were to lose the insurance, it wasn't likely to affect ABC's commitment to the series. It now airs three nights a week, and gives ABC bragging rights as the No. 1 network—with the substantial advertising revenue that comes with it.

In fact, ABC announced on Thursday that it was airing three more special editions of "Who Wants to Be a Millionaire" during the February ratings "sweeps."

There was a woman who worked at the Advocate in Stamford, Conn., where David Bauder had his first job. He remembers her well—how she used to yell at people on the phone.

"They had to deal with her because she covered education for the only newspaper in town," he says, "but they never really wanted to deal with her. And who knows what she missed by not treating people civilly and not being friendly. You try to be friendly and you try to be human with people. It doesn't mean that I won't have to do stories that anger them at times. It's my job."

Bauder is a nice guy in a cut-throat business. But it works for him.

He used to cover politics. Now he covers the television industry beat, with all its pressures: striving to develop sources, to master the complexities of telecommunications, to beat other reporters and avoid being beaten. And yet he is unflappable, low key, and—well, nice.

Which doesn't mean that he is not an aggressive reporter. He is. In fact, he got the story of "Who Wants to Be a Millionaire" and its insurance problems by going to a source and bluffing. And in doing so, he managed to get the story before a friend and competitor did.

Bauder stresses getting to know his sources. It takes a while. "You realize you're going to have some periods when you look ignorant and miss stories."

He is always trying to meet key people. Sometimes he goes out in the evening to industry events not because he expects to get a story but because he might make an important connection. He will call network sources and say, "Hey, I'm just poking around. I won't necessarily quote you on something like this, but just let me know what's going on, direct me in some way."

The tip for the "Millionaire" story, though, didn't come from one of Bauder's sources. A reporter in the AP's Washington bureau knew a lawyer in the insurance industry who had heard that the insurance company for "Millionaire" was trying to get out of its contract.

Bauder was interested. "Millionaire," of course, was a television phenomenon, attracting enormous audiences and changing the network landscape. In its wake, the networks were rushing to put more game shows and reality shows on the air. But from the beginning there were those who complained that the questions posed to contestants were too easy, and the insurance company seemed to agree. Obviously, newspapers would use this story.

To Bauder this was also an example of the diversity of his beat. He recalls that after 10 years of covering politics, he was beginning to burn out because "there are so many stories that are the same year after year." He can't imagine that happening with television.

"Television reflects life itself. Consequently, there are all sorts of stories you can do about things. You can write about it as a business, you can write about entertainment phenomena like 'Millionaire.' . . . I'm very interested in the news divisions, how they cover politics and things like that. It's a very wide variety of things in an industry that means a lot to people because it affects so many people. I haven't gotten bored with it for that reason. There's too much going on, frankly, for me to be bored with it."

There are some similarities to politics: "Some of the people in the TV industry are very political and knowledgeable about how they are seen in the public light. I found, oddly enough, that particularly when I cover TV news divisions, it's harder to get straight answers sometimes and information from them than it is from politicians. Because they're newspeople themselves; they're deeply suspicious of other newspeople and know all the tricks to avoid getting out particular information."

"Millionaire," though, was an entertainment story. The problem was that Bauder didn't know much. "We were kind of flying blind," he says. He knew that he could go to ABC for information, of course, but that would not have been wise: "I didn't want to call the network right off the bat because I didn't want to tip them off that quickly." ABC might have put out the story in a way that better served its purposes, perhaps leaking it to a less skeptical reporter, for example.

So with the hazy idea that the suit might have been filed in New York or Los Angeles, Bauder asked the AP's court reporters in those cities to see whether they could find the court papers. These are busy people, and it took a few days for them to take up Bauder's request. They found nothing.

In the meantime Bauder tracked down a spokesperson for the insurance company in London. "They were completely unhelpful. They wouldn't tell me anything. . . . They would have nothing to do with getting the story out." At about the same time, the pressure increased when he heard that Harry, his old city editor, now a reporter for the Long Island newspaper Newsday, was working on the same story. If Bauder wanted to get the story first, he had to get it now.

"I was just kind of going blindly, calling a bunch of people, when I managed to get a hold of a fellow from the Insurance Information Institute. He was my angel in this story. He knew everything about it. But he couldn't be quoted," Bauder says.

The source was willing to speak on background, meaning that Bauder could report what he said but could not quote him or even quote "an anonymous source in the insurance industry." All Bauder could do was report what the source told him without attri-

bution, as fact. And Bauder was unwilling to do that without confirming the information with at least one other reliable source.

Still, this was a very useful source: "He told me exactly what the case was; he gave me background about how the insurance worked and things like that." The one thing the source did not know was where the suit had been filed, although he had a few ideas, including the High Court of Justice in London, which was in fact the correct answer.

But by the time Bauder had figured that out, it was 4 p.m. in New York, 9 p.m. in London, and the chances of getting anything out of the court at that hour were zero. "I was kind of flummoxed," he says. He had everything he needed to write a story except for on-the-record confirmation that a suit had been filed.

At that point he called ABC spokeswoman Julie Hoover, "and I kind of did a little bit of a bluff," he says. "I said, 'Listen, I know what's going on here. I know what the story is.' I told them what I knew, basically. I didn't tell them that I didn't really have the story. I said, 'Listen, you know, I'm writing a story on this thing.

This kind of thing is going to get out. Can you help with this?'

"And they called me back 15 or 20 minutes later and faxed me the court papers and gave me a comment. I was able to nail everything down.

"I don't think that ABC was necessarily anxious to have the story out, because it's a little bit embarrassing about one of their biggest properties, their hottest show. But it's a story that reflects more poorly on the insurance company than it does on ABC, frankly. So I think that was part of their motivation for finally coming forward. Perhaps she also knew that it was going to be out in Newsday at some point."

It took Bauder about 45 minutes to write the story, with numerous telephone interruptions. "It's not a breaking story in the sense of a plane crash or something like that," he says, "but it was about 5 or 6 o'clock in the afternoon, and you know that's a time when editors and newspapers are meeting and putting together their pages and stuff like that, looking to see what's news. You don't want a story like that to go out too late, where they're going to miss putting it in the paper."

In his writing Bauder makes a point of including enough background about each story. He needs to explain "Who Wants to Be a Millionaire" to anybody who has not been following its success, who does not know its impact on the industry or the country. "You might assume that people know more than they know, which you really can't do," he explains.

Bauder is a fast writer, and he's also prolific; there are days when he will write four or five stories for the national wire. To add to his responsibilities, he also often writes about the music industry, mostly for his own enjoyment. He does it, he says, by planning his days and his time while adjusting to breaking events. He enjoys writing on a deadline; he gets a real rush from covering the Emmy or Grammy awards, but he sometimes finds it hard to explain why: "You've got to write through a story seven or eight times; you've got to keep your eye on the big picture of what's happening while it's happening and get it out really quickly, knowing that what you're writing is essentially going to lead the coverage for the country."

The "Millionaire" story was on the wire by 6:30 p.m. Newsday played its own story on Page 3, though it was no longer an exclusive. He talked to his old friend Harry "a couple of days after that, and he said it had gotten very depressing right around that time. He was a little bit bummed."

Bauder has been beaten on stories. Sometimes a source—for his or her own reasons—may prefer to give the story to another news organization. Bauder is unhappy but tries not to let it bother him too much: "I try not to get too worried about the stuff that's completely out of my control."

What really bothers him is when he knows about a story—read a report, attended an event—and misses an angle. "There was a story there that somebody else did that was better than you did. Or they had seen something that you hadn't seen. That's where it really drives me crazy. It really upsets me."

There are other less than pleasant moments on a beat. There are complaints from people and organizations he has written about.

"They call you up, and they scream at you a lot of times. I never try to ignore those calls. If I get them, I deal with them and I let them talk as much as possible. I'll explain my point of view—why I wrote what I wrote. I never try to stay away from those conversations, I never try to hide from those conversations, because I think I owe that time to sources. It doesn't mean I back down. If I do something wrong, I'll acknowledge it and try to correct it. But if I do something right that they disagree with, I say, 'Hey, we'll just have to disagree.'

"There are some people—and it annoys me—there are some people at networks who take things personally. They think you're out to get them or their network or something like that. And I've got to explain to them, no, sometimes I'm going to have to write things that are going to reflect poorly on your company, because it's news."

Still, he would not exchange his beat for general assignment work.

"I do like working beats," he says. "I like having the defined set of responsibilities. I consider myself somewhat of a self-starter—I like to plan out stories that I like to do and be watching for things that are good stories.

It's a little more difficult, obviously, doing that when you're general assignment because you're coming in and you're accepting what gets handed to you and what somebody else thinks is the big story of the day. On a beat, you're generating things through your own knowledge."

And on a beat, you can make life miserable for your old friend Harry.

12 Covering a Beat: Politics

N.Y.C. Mayor Drops Out of Senate Race

By MARC HUMBERT
Associated Press Writer

ALBANY, N.Y. (AP)—New York City Mayor Rudolph Giuliani has decided to drop out of the U.S. Senate race against Hillary Rodham Clinton, Republicans close to the mayor said today.

"The mayor will announce today he will drop out," a source said, speaking on condition of anonymity.

There was no immediate comment from the mayor.

Giuliani, plagued by health and marital problems, has been weighing his political future for three weeks.

Republicans in New York City and Albany got telephone calls from the mayor. Several of them, speaking on condition they not be identified, said the mayor told them he wasn't running because of concerns over his health. One of the Republicans said the mayor said he had still not decided on a course of treatment for his prostate cancer.

The first lady, in Brooklyn for a campaign appearance, said, "I will wait until we know for sure. . . . I don't do anything different because of that. I try to do what I have done for many months now."

"I have no control or say over what happens on the other side," she said.

Another GOP official, also close to the mayor and helping to prepare for the news conference, said Giuliani planned to attribute his decision to his health. He is telling Republicans that "he can't devote his full attention to the race," the official said.

There was no immediate word on whether Giuliani would endorse someone or what he does with his campaign cash.

Three weeks ago, the 55-year-old mayor announced he was suffering from prostate cancer and wasn't certain if he could continue in the Senate race. He

---

said the political decision would hinge largely on his determination about how to treat his cancer and whether he would be able to campaign effectively while undergoing and recovering from that.

But since his cancer announcement, the married mayor also went public with confirmation that he was seeing Judith Nathan, who he described as "a very good friend." He later said that he and his wife of 16 years, Donna Hanover, were discussing a formal separation.

Republican leaders will have to scramble to come up with a replacement candidate. The state GOP nominating convention is May 30 in Buffalo.

But Republican leaders, including Gov. George Pataki, had passed the word that if the mayor bowed out of the race, their favored candidate to take on the first lady would be Rep. Rick Lazio of Long Island.

The 42-year-old Lazio, now in his fourth term in Congress, had said that he would make no statement about his intentions until Giuliani made his decision. The congressman, who has about $3.5 million in his campaign bank account, had been preparing to run for the Senate until August when Pataki endorsed the mayor's bid and asked Lazio to suspend his effort. Lazio did so.

Calls to Lazio's offices in Washington and on Long Island today were not immediately returned.

Rep. Peter King and Wall Street multimillionaire Ted Forstmann had also expressed interest in running if Giuliani dropped out.

Marc Humbert was driving a school bus when he came looking for a job at the AP.

He hadn't always been a bus driver. A few years earlier he had worked as a reporter for the Saratogian in Saratoga Springs, N.Y., covering City Hall, government and politics. He had always had two loves: writing and politics. The latter was almost genetic; his parents were political, with his father serving as a Democratic committeeman in New York's St. Lawrence County.

But he wanted to give his other love, writing, a chance, and so he left journalism. "I went off to write the great American novel, and it turned out not to be," he says wryly.

He was driving a bus to put food on the table when he walked in off the street to the AP to talk to Ed Staats, the Albany, N.Y., bureau chief.

"He said he was fascinated by my resume. And he hired me," Humbert says.

Thus began the career of one of the AP's best political reporters, although he certainly wasn't that good at the start. Nobody is.

"You learn very quickly that you're new to the game and

nobody knows you," he says. "When you're first starting out, it's very hard. You don't know the players. You don't even know who they are. It's that murky area behind the politicians, their operatives. Over the years, you get to know who they are and you get to know who you can trust."

And over the years you get to know how to deal with sources. Because if money is the mother's milk of politics, sources play a similar role in political reporting.

"Source development is critical in covering politics," Humbert says. "It's such an insular type of society. There's this inner core of people who know what the hell is going on at any given time. Over time, you have to develop relationships with these people and get to know them."

It was Humbert's ability to develop sources that helped him break the news that Rudolph Giuliani was dropping out of the race for the U.S. Senate from New York in 2000. That campaign was the greatest story in Humbert's more than 20 years at the AP, and Giuliani's exit from the race was one of his biggest scoops.

It was harder than it looked. In any campaign it is important to identify early on those advisers and friends of the candidate who are willing to talk candidly about what's going on, sources beyond the official spokesmen or spokeswomen. Over months, each side feels the other out. Can you trust the source? Can the source trust you?

This was particularly difficult in the case of the Giuliani campaign. The mayor's inner circle was fiercely loyal and protective of the candidate. Giuliani and his top advisers tended to be distrustful and dismissive of the media, and some—including his press secretary, Sunny Mindel—were downright hostile to the press.

But Humbert found that a few people around the mayor were receptive after a great deal of coaxing.

"There is no secret to that," he says. "Ask how they feel about what is happening. What is their life like because of it all? Talk about sports, about the weather, about books, about movies. Talk about something other than the campaign. Gradually, a few of those around the mayor began to open up."

This is hard work—"To succeed in this business you've got to get up early, get in early, and stay late. There's no other way to do it."—but to Humbert, it's not unpleasant work. "I think it was I.F. Stone who once said, 'I've met very few politicians I didn't like or any I would trust.' . . . They're generally an interesting group of people, and I enjoy talking with them."

Talk with Humbert about sources, and inevitably the conversation turns to the question of anonymity. The AP's rule is straightforward: Anonymous sources may be used only when they offer fact—not opinion—that can be obtained only in that manner, and only if they refuse to be quoted on the record.

"Sometimes that can be frustrating," Humbert says. "There's some really good stuff that doesn't see the light of day," although some of it will wind up in print in newspapers that are less particular. "It's too bad in some ways but generally a very good rule."

He tries, where possible, to give the context of an anonymous quote: "Even if you can't say that it came from X candidate's campaign, you can say that the information would obviously hurt so-and-so's campaign, thus helping so-and-so's."

Sometimes he's tempted to violate the anonymity rule, and "sometimes I have and have heard about it. There are some things that are too good, so let's wink and nod and put it out there. You can sometimes argue about what's factual and what isn't, and then you get into that gray area—'It's almost factual. It's sort of factual if you look at it in this way.' "

There were no such questions about the Giuliani story, which really began on April 27, when the mayor announced that he had been diagnosed with prostate cancer and was undecided about what sort of treatment he would undergo and whether he would stay in the Senate race. "From then on it was a matter of checking with a half dozen or so good sources a couple of times every day."

On May 13 Humbert was able to report, based on conversations with "a person very knowledgeable about the discussions," that the mayor had been closeted with advisers the day before and "had sounded increasingly discouraged about the prospects for his campaign. The source said that pessimism was reflected in 'the type of questions that he's asking and the kinds of comments he's making after we give him answers.' "

On May 15 Giuliani canceled a fund-raising trip to California that was supposed to take place over the next two days. Still no decision on whether to stay in the race, said Humbert's sources. One very reliable source said the next day, "I'm getting the feeling, and it's just a gut feeling right now, that he is not going to run." This from a source who previously had been optimistic that Giuliani would persevere.

At 11 a.m. on Friday, May 19, Humbert got through to one of his sources close to Giuliani, a top adviser to the mayor. The source was now convinced that the mayor was not going to run and planned to announce soon that he would leave the race. No, he said, he had not spoken to the mayor directly, but he would be meeting with him shortly and would call Humbert immediately afterward. Humbert consulted with Sam Boyle, the New York City bureau chief; they talked with the national desk. The decision was made not to put anything on the wire until the source got back to Humbert.

The source called shortly after 12:30 p.m. The story hit the wire at 12:49 p.m., and by 1:45 p.m. AP had written through the story to update it with top New York Republicans receiving calls from the mayor notifying them of his decision not to run.

It doesn't always work that way, of course. Sometimes sources are not helpful, and Humbert—a bearish man, generally amiable though an aggressive reporter—has to get tough.

"Sometimes you have to. You develop a relationship with them over the years, talking about politics and other things, but at some point you just have to say, 'Come on. Don't give me any crap. I've been in this business long enough, you've been in this business long enough, just tell me the truth.' "

There are also occasions when a source will take a story elsewhere, to a competitor. Then Humbert will call to express his unhappiness. But that's it.

"Some reporters will say, 'I'm going to get you. I'm going to make you look bad.' But you can't do that. Because politics goes on. There's a continuum. You're going to have to deal with these people—you may have a fight with them on

some issue, and angry words are exchanged, but the fact of the matter is you can't just go out and try to get even. . . . You've got to play it down the middle. Especially with AP"—and its tradition of objectivity—"you've really got to do that."

Which is not to say that Humbert has no recourse. Sources often have their own pet stories. If an unhelpful source wants the AP to run a marginal story, Humbert says, "something that can be a 500-word story or a 200-word story or a 150-word story could turn out to be a 150-word story" when he writes it.

In the years since Humbert got off the bus he has had many successes and, like any reporter, some failures. He recalls the time he was writing about the appointment of a new judge who was replacing another judge. Humbert thought that the incumbent had died; he called the governor's secretary to make certain. She put him on hold for a couple of minutes and then picked up the phone and said, "Yup. That was it. He died."

A couple of days later Humbert got a call from the old judge's wife. She had seen the AP story when it had appeared in The New York Times. Her husband, she said, was very much alive.

"Fortunately, he's in the hospital, and he's really out of it and he didn't see" the story, she said.

"That's good. I'm so sorry," Humbert said.

Humbert wrote a corrective, which corrects a mistake in a previous story. AP asks papers that used the erroneous article to print the corrective; the Times did that a couple of days later.

By that time, of course, the judge WAS dead.

"That was the worst," says Humbert. "That was the absolute worst."

The best, he says, was a campaign that featured the first presidential spouse to seek public office.

"It was so intense," he says. "You've got Rudy Giuliani and Hillary Clinton, and you've got Giuliani getting cancer, and breaking up with his wife, and another woman. . . . Then you get this other Republican, this replacement candidate, and it turns out he can raise 30, 40 million dollars. It went on and on, day in and day out, always something new.

"And from the standpoint of being a reporter, the instant gratification that we reporters love, wire-service reporters, there it was—the A wire, every day almost.

"It was also a fascinating campaign to cover because there were some of the best operatives in the business working on this one. This wasn't your normal Senate campaign. This was people coming from Washington who had real connections. The old Clinton presidential hands, that sort of thing. You were also working against some of the best reporters in the business. That also made it fun. . . .

"And of course, it was fun being able to whup 'em now and then."

13 Working in Washington

Ross Perot's Nixon Connection

By JOHN SOLOMON
Associated Press Writer

WASHINGTON (AP)—Twenty-year-old White House papers say that Ross Perot pledged $60 million to help polish the political image of then-President Nixon. The offers tantalized Nixon aides, whose memos indicate they provided White House favors to Perot and his family.

Perot never actually put up any public-image money, and Nixon aide Charles Colson later described one Perot pledge as a "con job" designed to parlay access to the president.

Perot, suddenly in the spotlight as he ponders an independent bid for president, says he never made the $60 million in offers. Quite to the contrary, he said Nixon aides would sometimes solicit him with "fantasyland numbers . . . and beautiful and strange ideas. And I always made it very clear to them I wasn't interested."

Key Nixon aides remember it differently. Their memos are often rich in detail, conveying occasional frustration in working with Perot. Nixon declined to answer questions about his meetings with Perot.

An Associated Press review of Nixon-era documents in the National Archives show frequent contacts involving Perot, including White House intervention for Perot at the IRS and in two appeals of government contracts for his Electronic Data Systems computer firm.

The documents indicate the Nixon administration considered Perot one of its "financial angels" who should be "stroked from time to time."

Such White House attention is legal and perhaps routinely provided to major supporters and contributors, and there is no indication in the documents that Perot sought favors for money. Some memos go out of their way to describe administration decisions favorable to Perot as made solely "on the merits."

Office logs indicate that one Nixon assistant, Peter M. Flanigan, talked or met with Perot 40 times during his White House years. Flanigan says he remembers a man quite different than the fledgling independent presidential candidate who now declares himself a political outsider and rails against those who lobby Congress and the White House.

"This business about him being an outsider is nonsense," Flanigan says now. "He knows how to play every instrument in that band. He was the ultimate insider."

In private meetings with Nixon, according to White House memos, Perot offered $50 million for a public relations effort in 1969 that included plans to buy a major newspaper and television network and $10 million in 1970 to create a pro-Nixon think tank.

Nixon accepted both offers, but Perot never delivered, according to the documents. In 1971, the documents say, Nixon encouraged Perot to invest in a failing Wall Street stock brokerage, duPont Glore Forgan, and Perot did so, for $55 million. Perot lost millions in the brokerage house before it filed for bankruptcy.

A six-page memo prepared for Nixon's chief of staff H.R. Haldeman on Jan. 12, 1972, recounts a series of Perot complaints and requests for personal favors. The document describes White House efforts to intervene with federal agencies on behalf of Perot or EDS.

Perot on Wednesday said 99 percent of his contact with the Nixon administration involved his efforts to win freedom for American POWs in Vietnam, though he acknowledged seeking and receiving a few personal favors.

But Haldeman said in an interview that he vividly remembers Perot initiating the public-image offers, particularly $50 million to buy news media outlets, because Nixon was excited at the possibility "there would be one medium interested in our side of the story."

Colson, Nixon's special counsel who went to prison for obstructing justice, said in a 1988 oral history interview, "I don't know anybody in the whole four years I was at the White House who was able to muscle himself in quicker into the president's own confidence."

The Nixon archive documents say that between 1969 and 1973 Perot requested meetings with Nixon several times, received at least three private meetings with him, attended eight White House social events and sometimes had contact with the White House as frequently as once a week.

Former EDS President Milledge A. Hart III, in an interview, said Perot's ties allowed the company to use the White House as a "court of last resort" in disputes with agencies, but even when the company complained, "damn little happened."

Haldeman, who went to prison for Watergate misdeeds, acknowledged the White House occasionally intervened with government agencies because "a lot of our supporters weren't getting fair shakes."

"We'd simply make a point of asking for a review of the case to be sure . . .

proper action was being taken," Haldeman said in an interview on Monday. In that respect, Haldeman said, Perot was no different than hundreds of other business and community leaders with access to the White House.

What set Perot apart, Haldeman recalled, was his bold promises in meetings with Nixon to bankroll projects that would boost the president's popularity.

Colson, assigned to the think-tank project, said he set up the entire apparatus but when it came time to get the check, Perot stalled and then withdrew the offer.

"It was one of the most effective con jobs I ever saw in the White House. . . . He never put up a nickel. He parlayed that offer . . . into access, which ended up costing him nothing," Colson said.

In May 1969, Perot had his first private meeting with Nixon after he offered $50 million of his money "to spend for the benefit of the president," according to a memo by White House deputy Gordon Strachan.

The president suggested Perot buy some news media outlets, including the ABC network and the Washington Star newspaper, the memos said. The White House was so engrossed that counselor John Ehrlichman asked Flanigan to check out the value of ABC. "For your information," Ehrlichman wrote in a May 1969 memo, "ABC network is worth $400 million."

Perot denied ever making either the $50 million or $10 million pledges. When asked why they showed up in the documents he said: "I can't control what people scribble on pads."

"At no time did I bring up ever a $50 million program or did we ever have a conversation about a $50 million program for the president. That's just something floating out there in space," Perot said.

While Perot insists his contacts with the White House generally were limited to his well publicized efforts to free POWS, most of the favors detailed in White House memos involved personal or business matters.

Perot sought and received a number of personal favors, including autographed photos of Nixon, clearance for his son to see the Apollo 11 launch and a spot for his mother at a presidential prayer breakfast.

The archive memos said the administration also:

- Intervened with the Internal Revenue Service after the agency questioned Perot's deduction of a political contribution to Nixon's 1968 campaign on his corporate tax return. "The administration was modestly helpful" in reaching a settlement, according to the January 1972 memo written to Haldeman by Strachan.
- "Tried to intercede on Perot's behalf" after EDS lost a data-processing contract for Medicare claims in California. The Strachan memo said the loss of the contract, valued at $1 million, was "a legiti-

mate complaint" but the administration "became involved too late to turn it around without inordinate flak."

- Helped release a $400,000 payment that the Social Security Administration was withholding from Perot's company, alleging it had overcharged the government for processing of Texas Medicare claims. A draft of the Strachan memo states the administration "on merits determined Perot should receive the money."

- Awarded Perot a $62,500 contract without competitive bidding to study computerizing Medicare records. At the time, any contract worth $10,000 or more was subject to bidding.

By JOHN SOLOMON
Associated Press Writer

WASHINGTON (AP)—No favor was too small for billionaire Ross Perot to seek from the Nixon White House, which scrambled to keep one of its "financial angels" satisfied, Nixon-era documents suggest.

Perot called one Nixon aide at 11:15 p.m. to ensure his mother got into an upcoming presidential prayer breakfast, one memo shows.

Less than a month after a Nixon campaign staffer told the White House "Perot was a bit miffed" about a perceived slight, the administration devised a seven-point plan so that "Perot's problems with us diminish," other documents reveal.

The action plan included designating a White House staffer to talk with Perot occasionally and resolving Perot's complaint that he had received a "standard machine" photo of Nixon.

The White House then sent two personally autographed photos to Perot, who responded with a letter of thanks, documents at the National Archives show. Perot this week said he did not seek the photographs and speculated that an employee had submitted the request under his name.

Perot's draw on the attention of the Nixon White House began after he dispatched seven of his computer company's employees to work for the Nixon campaign in 1968. The contribution landed him on a list of substantial supporters dubbed "financial angels" who should be "stroked from time to time," memos show.

These supporters received White House briefing memos on issues such as the economy, special limited-edition copies of Nixon's inaugural address and, in Perot's case, eight invitations to White House social events, the records show.

One handwritten White House memo shows that Perot was recommended to "be placed at the top of the list for a commission." He was subsequently appointed to the Naval Academy's Board of Visitors by Nixon and served as the board's chairman.

"That's the type of plum appointment we reserved for people like him," recalled former Nixon chief of staff H.R. Haldeman.

Perot said he does not recall most of the contacts mentioned in the White House documents.

He said his dealings with the Nixon administration were generally limited to POW issues although he would "plead guilty" to seeking a few minor favors. For example, he once sought White House clearance so his son could watch the Apollo 11 launch.

White House aides said Perot's support of Nixon gave him unique access.

"If Ross Perot wanted to come in and see Richard Nixon, we probably tried to find a way if it were possible to accommodate him because he had been helpful and because he was a continuing supporter," recalled Dwight Chapin, Nixon's scheduling secretary at the White House.

When Perot became "hopping mad" that his request for a private meeting with Nixon to discuss POW issues in November 1970 had gone unanswered, an aide urged that a session be set up immediately, memos show.

Perot, the aide added, "is giving us one more chance to have him in for a brief chat with the president," the memo said.

In April 1969, the White House came to Perot's aid when he had trouble getting the Army Corps of Engineers to renew a lease on some of his property.

The White House sent a memo to the corps calling their attention to the fact that Perot was a "most substantial Nixon backer" and was "extremely interested in having this lease approved." The word "extremely" was underlined.

The files don't indicate how the appeal was resolved but a letter dated May 6, 1969, from Perot suggests he received a special meeting with the corps "to resolve this problem."

Perot said the meeting proved no help and eventually he settled the matter in court.

Ross Perot couldn't figure it out. How had John Solomon found out about his dealings with the Nixon White House? Had he been tipped off by one of those Republican "stealth agents"?

No, Solomon replied. His original source was . . . Perot.

It was 1992. Solomon wasn't one of the boys on the bus, following the candidates in that year's presidential campaign; he was a 24-year-old reporter who had made a name for himself at the AP in Milwaukee with a story about teachers who were allowed to return to the classroom after molesting pupils. In Washington he was assigned to the campaign finance beat. Freed of the responsibility of covering the daily campaign story, Solomon could take the time to report in depth.

In mid-April, Solomon asked Perot about his pattern of political contributions dating back to 1976, the first year for which Federal Election Commission records of donations are available. The Texas billionaire asked Solomon to define the period he was interested in. Solomon told him it was 1976 through 1992.

"So nothing before 1976, then?" Perot asked.

Interesting, Solomon thought. Was there something BEFORE 1976 that might be newsworthy? Solomon decided that the best place to look was the National Archives' Nixon document collection. He went there hoping to find a record of donations. He found a much larger story.

At that time Perot was at the height of his popularity, a self-described Washington outsider who looked like he could bedevil the two-party system and win the White House as an independent. As a potential independent presidential candidate, Perot had painted himself as a political outsider who quipped that he wouldn't "drink the water" in Washington.

But the documents at the National Archives told a different story—about a man who offered $60 million to improve Nixon's image, bought a failing Wall Street firm at Nixon's urging, and requested and received favors from the White House ranging from VIP treatment for his family to White House intervention with government agencies on behalf of his computer firm.

Solomon read through several exit interviews that Nixon aides gave when they left the White House, finding many details about Perot's efforts to curry favor.

He spent three days poring through dusty file boxes; most of the files for which he was looking were not indexed under Perot's name, and so the work was painstaking and often involved following the paths of different memos. The library closed at 4 p.m.; at that point he would return to the office to make phone calls for the story, tracking down former Nixon aides everywhere.

He reached H.R. Haldeman at a pub while on vacation in England. He reached John Ehrlichman at his new office in Atlanta, Peter Flanigan on his car phone in New York City traffic, and Charles Colson on a business trip in Michigan. Elliot Richardson stopped mowing his lawn on a Saturday afternoon to talk.

Many of them said they would only talk anonymously. "If you don't want to talk to me on the record, I'll go somewhere else," Solomon said.

"This was 20-year-old stuff," he says. "There was no reason to go off the record."

He was adamant, and in every case they agreed to be named as sources.

This has been Solomon's experience. Not long ago he was speaking to a lawyer who insisted on going off the record; Solomon literally walked out of the office. The lawyer called a half-hour later and agreed to be interviewed for attribution.

Again and again he has found that the first impulse of the politicians and government officials he deals with is to talk on background; faced with a reporter who insists on using their names, they will acquiesce. He notes that there are obvious occasions when a source has reason to be anonymous. An example: When he was covering the scandals involving President Bill Clinton and White House intern Monica Lewinsky, sources couldn't be quoted for fear of running afoul of a court-imposed gag order.

Getting people to talk on the record is important, Solomon says, if for no other reason than that he then can prevent them from using anonymity as a shield "so they can stab other people in the back."

When he arrived in the capital, Solomon marveled at "the sophistication of the game in Washington. People will have motives for what they say, and they will be deep-rooted. And the least likely source for a story may come through for you." It takes three or four years, he says, to learn where you should turn for information and learn how to avoid the pitfalls. Washington sources "know all the tricks, they know how to use us. You've got to avoid being duped," he says.

At the same time, Washington is perhaps the most competitive place in the world to be a journalist. The best reporters, Solomon says, "are inquiring, enterprising, and always looking for the next story." They are drawn to Washington by a fascination with government, with politics, and with intriguing personalities who hold great power in their hands.

Those people need not talk to Solomon. "There are 30 alternatives they can go to" with any story, he says. But Solomon assures sources that he will be fair, that he wants to know the whole story, and that he will take the time to get all sides to talk. That approach has worked throughout his career, when he has handled stories such as the Whitewater scandals, impeachment and campaign financing.

And it worked for the Perot stories. When Solomon called Perot for comment before the stories were transmitted, Perot returned the call within minutes, using the phone on his corporate jet. He was amazed to learn that he had scooped himself.

He did not hang up on the reporter. Instead, Solomon spent hours talking to Perot, his lawyers and his spokesmen, getting their side of the story. The effort paid off in a relationship that kept Perot talking even as Solomon produced several stories about his secret background as a Washington insider. Some of the best details about his relationship with Nixon came from Perot's own camp.

When Perot abruptly left the race in the summer of 1992, his former spokesman Jim Squires praised AP for its conduct in what was admittedly a series of tough stories that contributed to the billionaire's political demise. The stories won the Raymond Clapper Award for reporting.

And Perot kept talking to Solomon in the years that followed, often joking that he still could not believe that he had been the unintended source for Solomon's stories.

14 Reporting Overseas I

A Glimpse of Life in Post-Coup Zaire

By MORT ROSENBLUM
AP Special Correspondent

KISANGANI, Zaire (AP)—Euphoria is ebbing in Zairian rebel territory, born again as the Congo, and people desperate for a better life worry that Laurent Kabila, their liberator, may prove to be anything but their savior.

After three decades in obscurity, the 57-year-old career rebel is revealing an autocratic streak that casts doubt on his ability to share power and breathe life into one of the world's poorest nations.

"We want to eat, to find work, but first we need democracy," an unemployed schoolteacher says, pleading for anonymity on grounds that freedom of speech has yet to be demonstrated. "We're waiting."

With rumors rife Tuesday that beleaguered President Mobutu Sese Seko might quit the country, possibly for exile, Kabila's forces seemed poised to capture the remaining slice of Zaire not under their control.

But where Kabila is already dug in, the 57-year-old career rebel rules with a mix of messianic zeal and ad hoc absurdity. A seal on documents reads Democratic Republic of the Congo, the name Mobutu junked in 1971. In place of Mobutu's leopard symbol, there is, inexplicably, the lovable cartoon likeness of Simba, the Lion King.

But glimpses of life in liberated Zaire suggest no Disney fantasy.

In Goma, an 11-year-old swaggers about the airport in crisp camouflage. He pulls a 9 mm pistol and screams in Swahili at a British cameraman for wearing military boots. A 16-year-old persuades him to hold fire.

An officer inspecting an arriving passenger's belongings stares with suspicion at a packet of tissues. Convinced by a demonstration of their innocuous use, he next demands explanations for a safety razor.

Zairians learned long ago to mistrust government but to follow their president's example, pocketing public funds whenever possible. Kabila's first priority has been to alter such values. A harsh campaign against corruption slashed bribe-taking almost overnight, and a new Ministry of Spiritual Combat conducts reeducation programs.

Relief outweighs fear across the newly liberated territory, but the balance is shifting.

Rebel justice can be severe—some rebel soldiers have been whipped for minor infractions—raising worry that a brutal regime may replace a rotten one.

U.N. aid workers have decried mass graves in jungle areas of Zaire; they say Tutsis among the rebels massacred fleeing Hutu refugees from Rwanda. Most of the field workers believe Kabila condoned the killings, even if he did not order them.

While rebel spokesmen deny the massacre allegations, Kabila's men show little indulgence for refugees, near death and on the run. On Sunday, 91 people suffocated or were crushed to death because rebels crammed them so tightly into boxcars to send them home.

* * *

In Goma, the provisional capital captured six months ago, many are flatly impatient. Besides Mobutu's depredations, they endured the invasion of a million refugees and a cholera epidemic.

Entrepreneurs from neighboring Rwanda and Uganda, well funded and sometimes aided by officials of Kabila's rebel alliance, are taking over some businesses from local merchants.

"We are free of Mobutu, but there is still no work, no schools, no money," says Luc Namulolo, 35, trying to sell a few quarts of palm oil in a dirty yellow jerrycan at Goma's main market.

In Kisangani, the overwhelming mood is gratitude the hated tyrant is gone.

"A leopard, falling like that, it is unbelievable," says Bosco Zoinga, taking Mobutu's departure as foregone conclusion. "The change is night and day."

Zoinga's family built a comfortable hotel in 1973, as this once lovely colonial river crossroads began to slip into squalor.

It thrived despite theft and harassment by Mobutu's lieutenants. After unpaid troops ran amok and sacked the city in 1991, it nearly closed.

"They took the TV, the fridge, a car, then almost everything else," he says. "Until the revolution, the hotel was full of soldiers who paid nothing. Kabila saved us. Now we must see what happens next."

Soku Beaku nods grave agreement. He is an official money changer, once regularly cleaned out by police who levied instant fines for bogus offenses.

"You cannot describe how bad they were," he says. "Now the soldiers do not bother us. They give us required papers and enforce the law."

But his profession is a reliable bellwether. When Kabila's blitzkrieg buoyed spirits and aid workers and journalists dumped money into the economy, the value of the new zaire soared. Now, Beaku notes, it is slipping again.

* * *

Beaku, born in 1955 when Kisangani was the Belgians' rich garden city, Stanleyville, has seen too much not to be cautious. He has eight kids to raise.

He was 5 when independence came. Soon afterward he was hiding in the forest from leftist rebels, clad in leaves and heavily drugged, who randomly murdered with machetes and raped Belgian nuns.

Pierre Mulele led the rebels, who had supported slain Prime Minister Patrice Lumumba. Kabila was part of his movement.

The Congolese army called in mercenaries and Belgian paratroopers to put down the rebellion. Mobutu, then a colonel, was among Stanleyville's liberators.

In the resultant turmoil, Mobutu seized power with help from the CIA, who saw him as the key to unification. He stabilized the Congo, then looted it.

Kabila fought on from exile in Tanzania and, according to comrades, financed a comfortable life by smuggling gold, diamonds and coffee.

Now a triumphant conquerer, Kabila's philosophy is published in a 19-page tract, "Shipwreck of the Redemocratization Process." Though eloquent in its excoriation of Mobutu, it contains more ideology than ideas and offers no plan or coherent theory of government. The rhetoric harks back to Lumumba's unfocused populism.

Zaire's rich mineral deposits—and lucrative deals Kabila has struck with U.S. and European mining companies, giving the foreigners control of joint ventures—promise income for a new regime. But the victors face the gargantuan job of repairing a country that has almost entirely collapsed.

Kabila's spokesman, Raphael Ghenda, is vague about multiparty democracy. "We must first stabilize the situation, and that will take years," he says. When pressed, he suggests maybe four years.

* * *

Goma is getting to its feet. U.N. teams restored power and water. Fresh paint brightens such enterprises as the Chicago Bulls Hair Salon.

Kisangani is the other extreme. Jungle has reclaimed its outskirts. The port is a tangle of rusty metal. Streets are pocked, and buildings, black with decay, are crumbling.

Almost any conversation reveals human wreckage just as profound.

A strapping young man who calls himself Mr. John hounds foreigners for handouts. His last shirt is losing its left sleeve. His last straw is hope.

Rebuffed, he thrusts out his hand again: "Later?"

The first time Mort Rosenblum went to the Congo, he was a green young reporter. Literally.

He had grown up in Tucson and worked at the Arizona Daily Star. He'd always wanted to be a foreign reporter—"I never wanted to be a fireman, I never wanted to be an orthodontist, I just wanted to do this"—and so he joined the AP in 1965. "My first foreign posting was Newark, N.J.," he says. "Going from Tucson to Newark gave me more culture shock than going from New York to the Congo or anyplace since."

Most AP staffers who go abroad are first assigned to the international desk, editing foreign stories for American consumption or American stories for use overseas. Rosenblum transferred to the world desk and had been working there for six months when he went on a weekend excursion to Boston to visit his sister. There, he ate "a bad clam" and threw up most of the way back to New York.

"I just crashed and was asleep for about a half-hour when I got a call," he says. It was Jack Koehler, the AP's head of personnel. Michael Goldsmith, the AP correspondent in the Congo, had been

thrown out of the country for the fourth time, and Rosenblum would be his replacement.

"You've got two hours to catch the shuttle from Kennedy to Washington to pick up your Congo visa and get over to Brussels and down to Kinshasa," Koehler said.

And so, Rosenblum recalls, he packed in about an hour to go overseas for what would turn out to be a lifetime as a foreign correspondent. He arrived in Kinshasa at 4 a.m., still sick with food poisoning.

"I was 23 years old, sick and scared. . . . I figured if I got through that, everything else was up. I've never really been through anything worse."

But he's been through a lot. After his stint in Kinshasa he went to Lagos, where he covered the end of the Biafran war, and then to Singapore, where he was the bureau chief and reported on Vietnam. He was the bureau chief in Argentina during the Peron era ("I was on about seven death lists that I knew of") and then the Paris bureau chief. He left the AP to serve as the editor of the International Herald Tribune. He returned to the AP in 1981 and has been based in Paris ever since; his travels have taken him everywhere to cover wars, disasters, political upheaval.

The biggest single difference between reporting in the United States and reporting elsewhere, he says, is that here "just about everybody has a reason to talk to reporters. It's likely to bring them something good—either publicity or thrills or whatever it is. And most people, even if they don't want to talk, will talk. In most foreign countries it's the other way around. There's nothing good that's going to come to them from talking to reporters, and lots of bad things, including death, can come to them if they do."

This is how he does it: "You've got to make them feel that you understand the delicacy of their situation, what their situation is, and you're not going to get them in trouble. . . . You try to get a rapport going. It's why it's better to speak to people one on one. It's why it's important to know languages. You're always better off in a language they've spoken for a long time, because even if you're not so good at it, they express themselves a lot better."

Outside of Latin America, he says, French is a useful language to know; throughout much of Africa and Asia it was the language of the colonial masters, and it is still spoken by many in government.

He says: "You talk to them. You talk about general things; you try to let them understand that you know the political situation and the difficulties. You ask your questions in a very subtle way. You come sideways, mostly; you ask your questions diagonally. It's kind of like a crab walking. . . . There'll be times when I'll be talking to somebody and I'll make a not too obvious but clear gesture of closing the notebook and putting it on the table or putting it in my pocket and then ask him, 'Hey, what about this?' It somehow gives him a signal that you're slipping into confidences. And then, if he says something that you know will cause him trouble, you don't quote him on it."

The most difficult part of being a foreign correspondent, Rosenblum says, is not a matter of reporting: "The hardest job of a foreign correspondent is to cross these cultural bridges. You have to take the story from the cultural context in which it happens, take it across this cultural bridge, and explain it in terms of somebody who doesn't really know the larger context of the story.

"It's more of a writing problem than a reporting problem. If you've been a foreign correspondent for a while, you see the other culture, you live in the foreign culture. It's why, by the way, it's important to avoid this parachute journalism stuff. Reporters have to live in these societies and get to know not only people and the stories but the societies themselves, how people think."

He recalls the advice he once received from a veteran newspaper foreign editor: "Don't tell me what happened on a street in Chad. Tell me what the street looks like."

"It's sort of that. You have to put in road markers and put in the background and explain where things are coming from and why people think in ways they do," Rosenblum says.

But reporting also plays a role in translating a foreign culture for an American audience. Rosenblum fills his notebooks with details—the kind of material that tells readers more than paragraphs

of explanation could. He remembers that once in Nigeria he was writing about refugees streaming down the roads with all their belongings on their heads. Hugh Mulligan, long an extraordinary AP writer, taught Rosenblum a lesson: " 'No, no, no, no, no,' he said. 'Particularize, don't generalize. They're walking down the road with their mattresses, cooking pots. . . .' "

"There's not much I can do in life, but one thing is I've got a pretty good eye for detail," Rosenblum says. "And I think it's because I'm naturally curious. I like it; it's important to me. I look. I'm fairly attentive. I look for telling little details. And they really help the story along."

But Rosenblum's life as a foreign correspondent is not always a matter of subtleties and detail. He often is plunged into chaos and must rely on his wits to get the story—and to survive. This is his account of his return to the Congo three decades after he first went there as a food-poisoned neophyte:

Mobutu Sese Seko was teetering, and I hovered around waiting. After all, we'd both started our respective careers in Kinshasa in the mid-1960s, and I'd watched him develop as a supremely accomplished thieving, murdering dictator. I did not want to miss his final fireworks.

The alarm sounded late one afternoon while photographer Santiago Lyon and I were in Kisangani, a moldering Congo port at the bend in the river from which any exit requires time and luck. APTN [AP's television arm] colleagues solved one problem fast. They chartered a large plane from Nairobi.

The second problem was tougher: persuading the Italian pilot to overfly interminable jungle in the dead of night, with no official clearance, and head to Brazzaville, where chances were that he would be arrested and his aircraft would be seized. Not surprisingly for a veteran African bush pilot, he was ready to try it.

Brazzaville, when not in flames, can be an amusing town, but his boss ordered him to bring us back to Nairobi. Instead of flying three hours on a direct line to an airport just across the river from Kinshasa, we spent two days diverting via Paris. We caught the last Air France flight before the Ndjili airport closed, a mixed blessing. Few things I've seen since match my first moment as a foreign correspondent, landing in Kinshasa in the dead of night, faced with several dozen nonofficial officials all bent on extracting cash against nonspecific threats limited only by the traveler's imagination. In the intervening 30 years Ndjili had gotten far worse, but I'd gotten better at dealing with such situations.

A very large armed person I nicknamed Wacko took me and several colleagues in hand for what seemed like a bargain investment. Wacko, the son of a general, was prominent in pro-Mobutu circles, another mixed blessing. He made a terrific guide-bodyguard when not overly drunk. His demand for emoluments stayed within reason. At some point, however, I knew that Laurent Kabila's sudden entry into Kinshasa would make Wacko a seriously dangerous loose cannon.

The next problem was housing. Nearly everyone stayed in the Memling Hotel downtown on the theory that there is safety in numbers and because correspondents always seem to stick together in one place for no particular reason. With that in mind, I took a room at the Intercontinental in a diplomatic neighborhood. The place had a defensible perimeter, and AP would have backup headquarters in case, as I suspected, the Memling got too hairy.

Then there was transportation. On a tough story, a reporter is frighteningly dependent on a sturdy car with a spare tire, a gutsy and intelligent driver, and a reliable supply of gas. That took some doing. And communications. We had a satellite phone for filing, but I also rented a mobile that could direct-dial New York.

Each day brought a new surprise. Once the New York Times correspondent, reputed to have excellent contacts, burst into the Memling to warn us that he had heard that a paramilitary gang was headed over to rob and kill us all. Some precautions seemed in order. We were some sight, a hotel room full of reporters of every description cowering behind a mountain of furniture piled against the door. Someone outside rattled the doorknob, triggering a brief panic. It turned out, we later learned, to be the chambermaid.

I squirreled away enough supplies—water, food, fuel—to carry our little crew through a week of disruption. I made friends in high and low places, looked up people I'd known decades earlier, studied back routes and river landings. Mainly, I cruised "le cité," the sprawling slums where everything starts and finishes in Kinshasa.

Day after day, rumors and false alarms suggested that Mobutu had left Kinshasa, at least for his upriver jungle redoubt of Gbadolite. Then, one afternoon, a senior minister announced a news conference in the prime minister's backyard. I got up close and looked at the prepared notes scribbled, crossed out, rewritten—clearly the work of a rattled committee. Listening closely to the double-talk, I realized this was it. Two phrases said clearly that Mobutu was gone. To backstop, I checked with a British reporter I'd trusted for over 20 years, a man with long African experience. And then a German. Both had heard the same thing. I slipped away and, using that miracle mobile phone, dictated to New York. It took careful wording, but the essential message was plain.

CNN led with the story 10 minutes later, using our quotes. Eventually, on studying their own notes, other followed. But Kabila's troops were still out beyond the airport, held off by token resistance from Mobutu's ragtag army. French military sources were helpful, but no one had reliable details from the front. One morning I awoke to panic. It was nearly 7 a.m., and CNN's live banner announced, "Rebels enter Kinshasa." Well after midnight, when I'd last checked, they had still been at least 30 miles away. CNN, it seems, had jumped the gun.

But this was clearly the morning it would all come down. A small knot of loonies assembled in front of the Memling, and we had a rapid conversation all of us know well. We wanted to go up the road. We realized it was stupid and suicidal. We waited for the others to make a call. And it came out as it always does. Since most of us there respected the others' judgment and none of us wanted to appear chicken, we formed a three-car convoy and headed toward the airport.

As Kabila's troops advanced, fleeing Congolese would want three things: good vehicles in which to flee faster, convertible cash, and Americans or Europeans on whom to vent their anger. Our little convoy provided all three, via delivery service. Twice we roared through Congolese roadblocks before startled soldiers could shoot. We reached what amounted to the front and decided finally to get the hell out of there. By then, of course, it was too late. The other two cars turned around behind me. I swung my Geo Tracker jeep in a U-turn just as a Congolese captain shoved a gun barrel at the window. For the next 15 minutes we bounced over potholes and careered around corners in a car chase straight out of a bad movie. Next to me [New York Times reporter] Ray Bonner yelled, "Faster," as though I were dawdling in second gear. Finally, our pursuers fell behind for reasons I did not go back to verify.

By late morning rebels had entered the center of Kinshasa. There was little real fighting, but bullets flew everywhere. Shots were fired in celebration, in panic, in frustration, in sport. I took cover behind a thin metal sheet in the large open market by the Memling and called New York to describe the scene.

A young desk person seemed obsessed by repeating small details and taking his time. At one point he asked, "What's all that noise?"

"Gunfire," I told him.

"Isn't it dangerous?" he replied.

"Not for you," I said. "Can we just finish here?"

15 Reporting Overseas II

Where the Dead Speak Loudly

By LAURA KING
Associated Press Writer

PRISTINA, Yugoslavia (AP)— Kosovo is a land where the voices of the dead speak as loudly as those of the living—perhaps even louder.

The dead are nowhere and everywhere, some never to be found, others scattered in nameless graves, their bones heaped in the rubble of what were once pretty village homes, their last moments etched in the memories and the haunted faces of those who lived through what happened here.

Everyone, it seems, is on intimate terms with these dead. Nearly every village, every neighborhood, every family has been somehow touched by the savage spasm of killing whose dimensions are only becoming fully clear now, as NATO peacekeepers fan out across Kosovo and ethnic Albanian refugees flood back across the borders.

What the people of Kosovo are find-ing as they return to their homes is nothing less than a giant charnel house.

So far, the numbers are only esti-mates: Western military and humanitar-ian officials say upward of 10,000 people may have died in a concerted campaign of atrocities by Serb police, troops and paramilitary men—this in a province whose prewar population was put at about 2 million.

Over the past week, the reckoning has begun in earnest, as refugees—whose chaotic exodus from Kosovo over the past three months already represented the greatest mass displacement seen in Europe since World War II—come home and confront the proof of terrible doings in their absence, or in the midst of their flight.

They find it, at times, on their very doorsteps. Body parts clog family wells. In some village homes, corpses still lie

---

where people were cut down in the midst of ordinary tasks—cooking a meal, or watching a TV program.

Any plot of open land might have become a boneyard. Belongings lie scattered in rain-soaked gardens and on muddy roadsides: a teddy bear, a pink blouse, a bedroom slipper.

As returning neighbors find one another alive, they embrace and deliver stark news of disaster: I saw your brother. His body was burning. Or: Your cousin's throat was cut. Or: They made them lie on the ground, and then shot them. Your uncle was one.

"Murder is a folk art," the Yugoslav-born writer Charles Simic wrote in "Orphan Factory," a collection of poems and essays published last year. "They keep perfecting it without ever being pleased with the results."

* * *

Halit Shala, 42 and haggard, offers a wrist-first handshake, thumb clasped against his palm. It's what country people here will do when they want to greet someone, but are afraid their hands are not clean enough to offer.

Shala has been shaking hands that way since he came home from Albania last week and found a shallow grave in his family courtyard containing what he believes are the remains of eight people. Two of them, he thinks, are his brothers.

"If I didn't have faith in God," he said, shaking his head, "I would lose my mind." Shala lives in Velika Krusa, on the main road between the western Kosovo cities of Pec and Prizren. The town has a melancholy distinction: it was chosen for scrutiny by the International War Crimes Tribunal, and is named in the indictment against Yugoslav President Slobodan Milosevic.

The horror that Shala came home to is among the sites being investigated by forensic experts gathering evidence for the tribunal. On this day, though, investigators are busy with another site just down the hill and across the main road: a charred home where townspeople say dozens of bodies—perhaps 40 or 50—were incinerated by Serb police and paramilitary men after a killing spree in the town on March 27, three days after the NATO bombing of Yugoslavia began.

Paprika farmer Skender Duraku, a cousin of the family that owned the house, was hiding in a grove of bushes when police trucked the bodies to the house and set it ablaze, he said.

"We couldn't get close because of the smoke and the smell," he said, his eyes watering with the memory. "I never imagined this smell, the flesh of humans."

Behind plastic tape roping off the site, investigators were at work, wearing white protective suits, surgical masks and weary expressions. A pile of yellow evidence bags lay heaped outside the house. One investigator knelt to help another off with the plastic bags tied over his boots.

Duraku then went back into the house after the wreckage had cooled, trying to see which of his relatives might be among the dead. Townspeople had scattered in panic after the killings, and many in his extended family were unaccounted for.

"Of course we couldn't tell anything from what we saw—everything melted, mixed together, the house, the bones," he said. "You knew they were people, but who? How do we know? I didn't try to enter again."

Duraku said he didn't know if he could stay on his land and begin farming it again. From anywhere in his fields he can see the hulk of the house, itself a blackened skeleton. Even if it is torn down, he thinks his eyes will always be drawn to the spot.

"It's so hard," he said, "just to be here."

* * *

The killing in Kosovo simply unhinged some.

In Djakovica, scene of some of the most systematic of slaughters, many people saw family members killed before their eyes. Men, in hiding places because they knew they would be slaughtered if they were found, heard their wives being abused and their children beaten by police and soldiers.

"The city was dead," said Amaia Esparza of Doctors Without Borders, a France-based humanitarian group that began working in the city last week, shortly after the arrival of NATO troops. "And the people, they were dead too in a way, even the ones left living."

Her group came to Djakovica to assess healthcare needs and decided that among the most urgent was to set up a mental health project to begin individual and group counseling for the people of Djakovica.

"You have children who are like little zombies—not even sad, just empty, absent, gone to some other place," she said. "There are old people who just cry and cry. Young girls who were raped—I don't think they will ever talk about it, but their lives are ruined. And for the men it is terrible, because they wanted to protect their families from all of this, and they couldn't."

In the town of Junik, on the Albanian border, the dead were Salih Gjoda's chief companions. In his solitude, he thought of neighbors and relatives who had died, and sometimes spoke to them, he said, as if they were there.

For 10 days, Gjoda and his 13-year-old daughter Shkendije had been the only inhabitants of the town, little more than a cluster of wrecked houses at a bend in the road.

They became separated from the rest of the family in the crush to cross the Albanian border, and Gjoda's wife was wounded when their tractor convoy came under Serb attack. When he was at last able to find his daughter, they made their way back home to wait for others to return.

Late last week, they were still waiting. Gjoda, 59, who lost a leg to diabetes years ago, sat patiently on a plastic crate by the side of the road, his crutches propped up against the shattered storefront of his brother's tool shop.

The family home was burned, so he

and his daughter were sleeping in the store. Fighters from the rebel Kosovo Liberation Army stopped by now and then to give them a bit of bread.

"If only I could find something to cover the roof so the rain won't ruin everything we have," he said fretfully. The store was completely empty, picked clean by looters.

Around him, the village was a ruin. There was not a building in sight that had not been torched or shelled or shot up. The mosque's minaret was blasted. Water gushed from a broken pipe. Grunting pigs rooted aimlessly about.

On a wall was scrawled the Serbian word "umiri"—die.

Gjoda was wearing his eyeglasses upside down because one lens was broken, and he needed the remaining one for his weaker right eye. It gave him the same skewed, shattered look as everything else in sight.

He would be glad to see his neighbors when they returned, he said, but in the meantime he occupied his thoughts by remembering what the village was like before all this happened. And its people, as they had been, before all the killing.

"I have enough company," he said.

It was a horrible place, Kosovo. "That's the only story I think I've ever covered in which things were actually much, much, much worse than they looked on TV," says Laura King. The conditions were awful, the stories heartbreaking, the risks horrendous.

And yet, she says, "I felt so lucky to be there."

She had covered conflicts in the Middle East, where she had spent two years posted in Jerusalem. She was sent to Vienna for a month to help edit copy from the Balkans, and when the Kosovar Albanians began to flee from their Serbian tormentors, she spent two or three weeks in Macedonia, covering the refugee crisis. Then she was sent to Macedonia again, after the NATO bombing. When the alliance's troops went into the beleaguered province, King would go as well. She would have an opportunity to see for herself what had happened during the time of the bombing, when Western journalists left the country.

"I felt very fortunate to be able to witness it and try to write about it," she says.

"But I think like most journalists there, I felt that I just couldn't convey the magnitude of the destruction and the suffering that had taken place. . . . I guess there was just mainly a sense that it really needed to be written, it really needed to be written about in the best, fairest, most comprehensive way that each of us could manage. And we all felt that we were falling short every day."

But she also felt scared.

"Going in in a convoy with the NATO troops—that was actually pretty genuinely scary because there were still Serbs in the province, and nobody knew if there were going to be sniping at the convoy and whether there were land mines and things like that," she says.

In fact, "there were lots of mines and booby traps and unexploded ordnance around, so out in the countryside especially, if you were on some tangly, brambly path, it was very frightening. You couldn't see very well and didn't know if you were going to trip something off."

The fear mingled with horror: "We didn't really know what to expect. We knew there would be lots of destruction from the bombing and also from looting, but it was just so rare to see any kind of a scene where you didn't see some effect of what had happened—all kinds of burned-out wrecks of vehicles and just everything broken. . . . So many mass graves were being found because people were coming home and looking around their villages and finding lots and lots and lots of bodies."

Even aside from the story she was covering, the conditions were difficult. "Reporting and writing stories was always the easy part of the day," she says. The reporters' stories were sent to the AP by satellite telephone, and they struggled to get signals and hold them long enough to file their copy.

"The whole place had been so trashed during the Serb occupation, by the NATO bombing, and then by the Serbs themselves on the ground. Just about anywhere we could find to stay had been looted. We were staying in a couple of different apartments belonging to people who had some kind of connection to the AP: stringers or friends of them. . . .

"Most of them had had the electricity cut off. There would be a whole refrigerator full of completely rotted food, and often

Serbs would have come through, either soldiers or even neighbors, [and] clothes would be thrown out on the floor. Basically, it would look like the scene of a robbery with drawers pulled out and cupboards emptied and anything of value having been taken, a television, a stereo or something like that. It was very poignant—all these personal possessions all over the place.

"One apartment we stayed in had stayed safe and been locked up all that time, but all the others had been broken into and looted somehow. In each case we knew that the owners were going to be coming back soon and wanted to fix it up a little bit for them, so we would try to put some things away and get rid of all the horrible, rotten stuff in the refrigerator."

She recalls one particular apartment, the home of a stringer who had fled to Macedonia with his family but was returning in a few days. The streets were unsafe at night, and so the reporters spent their evenings trying to clean the flat, but "even after what we had done, they were so shocked when they came back, and they just started weeping when they saw the place," King says.

There was little food. "We brought in some water and some dried food, but that ran out pretty quickly. We really had trouble getting our hands on bottled water that was safe to drink. We were just eating a lot of crackers and peanut butter and stuff like that."

It was a long way from Montpelier, Vt., the tiny state capital where King started her AP career. She worked her way up to a place in the Washington bureau, the "kind of bureau that a lot of people see as an end in itself." But not King.

"I knew when I was in Washington that I really wanted to be elsewhere, out in the world. Because Washington was really insufferable at the time. Even more than now, it just really considered itself to be the center of the universe. It was so provincial. For a place where people tended to know a lot academically about foreign affairs, nobody seemed very interested about the lives of people elsewhere in the world."

She started over, transferring to New York and the international desk, where she worked the overnight and prepared to go overseas. She was posted first in Tokyo and then in Jerusalem.

Like others who cover stories overseas, King is aware that Americans are not always interested in foreign news. Refugee crises in Africa, for example, sometimes have been relegated to second-tier news in American papers. The Balkan story was different. American troops were involved. And perhaps unfortunately, King notes, there was interest in this story because the refugees were people to whom readers in the United States and elsewhere in Europe could relate. "A lot of the people who fled and who came back were middle-class people. They were doctors and writers and lawyers."

In Kosovo she worked with an interpreter, "a really wonderful young man" who had played the same role during her stints in Macedonia. He "knew the kinds of questions that I liked to ask and the way that I liked to ask them" and was good at giving responses word for word, unlike some interpreters, who will listen to a 10-minute answer and translate it as "Then they came home."

She also worked with an Albanian driver. In her last day in

Kosovo she was assigned to go to the border to pick up an AP "hard car," a car that had been armor-plated so that it was at least somewhat bulletproof. Unfortunately, the pickup point was changed; King and her driver ended up at an unmapped part of the border, and there was no sign that demarcated the line between Kosovo and Serbia. The line was an important one; across it were angry Serbs who had been humiliated by their retreat.

"We strayed over, and we hadn't realized that we had strayed over until we were stopped at a Serb checkpoint," she says.

"Of course we tried to stay very calm. It was the middle of the day, but there were a couple of guys, not really soldiers but kind of paramilitary-type guys who were very drunk and very belligerent, and one of them was waving a gun at my driver. I really thought that he might shoot him. Then I guess he'd have to shoot me, too," she says, laughing nervously even years later. It was, she says, "the closest I've ever been to feeling that somebody was going to be killed right in front of me."

But the moment passed, and King and her driver were taken to a police station, where they were questioned for a couple of hours before being allowed to leave.

They went back to Pristina, got on the satellite phone to determine the actual pickup point, and then got the hard car without incident. But because of all the time that had been lost, she was unable to polish her last story from Kosovo, the one that is printed here.

"I had a lot of notebook stuff that seemed quite powerful but hadn't found a way into a story," she says. "We were all writing spot stuff a couple times a day or spot features for same-day use, but I hadn't done anything that I thought came anywhere close to summing up what I'd been seeing."

She wrote it in just an hour. There was no lack of material.

"Everybody wanted to tell you their story. Everybody did. It's never been easier to solicit information than it was there, just because everybody had this tremendous need to talk to someone about what had happened," she says.

"It was exhausting at times, because sometimes you'd be out at the scene of some awful, awful thing, and talk at length to two or three or four people, and have enough for the story, but other people would be sort of crowding around, tugging your sleeve and wanting to tell you more. You couldn't turn away from somebody who was telling you about how a family member was killed in front of their eyes or how they came home and found a corpse in the house or something like that. But at some point you just had to disengage. That was hard.

"It was easy to get information. It was hard to know what to do with it."

16 Re-creating Reality: About Narrative Reconstructions

Journalists always say they're writing stories. Bruce DeSilva disagrees.

"We call everything stories that we do in journalism, but most of what we do is articles, and they wouldn't pass a 6- or 7-year-old kid's test for what a story is," says DeSilva, the head of AP Newsfeatures.

The stories DeSilva has in mind are like fairy tales or novels or the kinds of tales people tell each other in front of a fire. The difference is that they're true.

They have central characters. "The character has to be somebody who the reader is going to be emotionally invested in and care about in some way. You can love the character or you can detest him, which is a kind of caring. But there has to be an emotional investment," DeSilva says.

"That means there also has to be characterization. You can't just have name, job title and age as you usually do in a newspaper because you can't know somebody at all that way. The character has to be developed so he becomes a real person on the page."

The central character has to have a problem—a real problem that readers will take seriously. And the character must struggle to solve that problem: "That means the problem can't be easily resolvable, either. If the character has a problem and she solves it, you have a paragraph. You don't have a story."

Finally, you have to have a resolution.

"You have the character defeated by the problem or overcoming the problem. Real life isn't that neat, but there must be some kind of change. You can't have a character struggling and struggling and struggling right off the page with nothing happening. There has to be something that changes at the end that gives a sense of closure," DeSilva says.

Without these four things—character, problem, struggle and resolution—a narrative will not work.

"That's the bad news. The good news is an awful lot of things in life that happen, happen this way. They take this natural storytelling form. Because of that, the opportunities are everywhere.

"And if you start thinking in terms of storytelling instead of reporting the news, you'll see stories everywhere. Most of what we print in the newspaper is endings. We mostly print the resolutions of stories and tend not to tell the entire story. We just tell the ending. An election, a court verdict, a decision by a judge, a bankruptcy—all these kinds of things that we report as news usually are the resolution of what is in fact a much longer and very interesting story involving human beings struggling with life. If you start looking for stories, very often the place you find them is the resolution."

But why write these kinds of stories at all?

Because he says, "there is plenty of academic evidence that information given to people in this form—in the form of real storytelling—is more likely to be understood, read all the way through and remembered than any other way in which we can give people information. . . . It's entertaining, it's interesting, it can take things that are news that might otherwise be on the dull side and make them fascinating. Because of instead of just giving the bare, dry facts, you're dealing with the texture of people's lives and their struggles, and so it makes everything interesting.

"Additionally, it's a great explaining tool. There are certain kinds of stories that are simply impossible to understand until you tell a story about them. It's like, 'You're having trouble understanding this. Well, let me tell you a story. . . .' A story often, by way of example, explains how something happens."

An example: In the 1990s newspapers throughout New England wrote about the collapse of the real estate and banking market there. But the in-depth and complicated series often went unread; not so the story of a hot-dog vendor who started fixing up houses and selling them, succumbed to the banks' suggestions that he expand his real-estate operations, and finally ended up owing $300 million.

These kinds of stories require a special brand of reporting, DeSilva says.

"It does, although I wish it didn't so much. Because the kind of reporting that's done for narratives I wish found itself into other kinds of stories more than it does," he says.

First, the reporter has to know enough about the central character "so you can convey what that person is like—not by characterizing him by saying that he's smart or funny or whatever but by showing his behavior and speech in ways in which the character emerges.

"The character emerges through action and dialogue. Not quotes.

Quotes are what people who are being interviewed say to us, and they're often not very good at [revealing] character because people, acutely aware of being interviewed, often put a face forward which is what they want to be seen as instead of what they're like. Dialogue is what people are saying to each other in real life that we hear or reconstruct."

This is not to say that narratives should have long quotes: "Unless you have the actual words that were spoken, from having heard them or from some kind of recorded source, no long quotes in narratives. You quote only those things that could reasonably be expected to be remembered. . . . The quotes are only a few things like, 'Oh my God, I'm shot.' And not much more than that." The rest is paraphrased.

Second, the reporter has to be prepared to re-create a sense of the places that are central to the story. "You can't write a story without a setting," DeSilva says.

"Nobody's going to create a movie that's set nowhere. They're often set in a place, and the place is often really important for creating mood and helping you understand people and motives because place often has a powerful influence on people and how they behave. A sense of place means reporting what it's like there, what you see and hear and smell and taste that creates that sense of place on the page."

Finally, "you have to report the action. You have to report what people are doing with real detail. Again, using your senses to allow readers to see the action, so it unfolds in front of them. In narrative you don't tell people what happened. You allow them to experience what happened by scene writing. And you can only write scenes through detail. Through all the information as it comes through the senses. What you see and smell and hear and taste. Most journalists don't do much of that and often don't know how. People who are writing narrative have to relearn how to report so they can help the reader experience the world through the senses instead of just telling them what happened.

"It works, by the way, not only in reporting stories where you're present but also reporting stories where you're not present but you're interviewing people about what happened. You just need to ask the right questions. You have to ask people what they saw and heard and smelled."

17 Saving a Child

The Making of a Rescue: 17 Minutes of Terror

By CHELSEA J. CARTER
Associated Press Writer

TIFTON, Ga. (AP)—Four-year-old Ryan Eschleman was trapped in Grandma's car as it filled with the brackish, frigid water of the pond. On the other side of the rear window, a man pounded against the glass, desperately trying to break it.

Other would-be rescuers were in trouble nearby. A woman was floating, face down. Under the water, a man was unconscious, unseen, and a valiant policeman also struggled beneath the surface.

Ryan's knuckles were white as he clutched the headrest of the back seat.

Now the water was almost up to his neck.

* * *

When accidents happen on television, they often happen in slow motion—orchestrated, like a ballet.

But when accidents happen in real life, the world is helter-skelter. The most crucial minutes of Ryan Eschleman's young life were like that. There were 17 of them in all, and they were filled with chaos.

In those few minutes, six men and a woman put aside thoughts of their own safety to try to save a 4-year-old boy. You could call them heroes, but heroism was not their intention; sometimes in life, valor comes uninvited.

It was 11:28 a.m. on Tuesday, Feb. 11—a cool 40 degrees and sunny in this south Georgia town of about 16,000 residents.

Ryan's grandmother, Peggy Cardona, was running late for work as a hair stylist at the Total Image: Take 2 salon. She had two minutes to spare. She eased her light blue 1990 Nissan Stanza into the employee parking area behind Tifton Mall.

The parking spot was on the border of a well-manicured, grassy 40-foot incline that ended at the edge of a pond—a catch basin for rainwater, 150 yards long and as wide as a football field.

The Nissan's automatic gearshift was broken, so if she put it in park, it was impossible to change gears. She was used to leaving the car in neutral and setting the emergency brake. This time, she forgot.

Ms. Cardona reached to open the back door for Ryan when the car lurched forward and started to roll. It picked up speed as it moved down the slope. It slid effortlessly, almost gracefully, into the pond.

"Nana! Nana! Nana!" Ryan screamed. He craned his neck for a glimpse of Grandma. She was gone.

* * *

Devin Batten, 23, was in the mauve stylist's chair waiting for Ms. Cardona. Lanky, with a shock of dark hair, Batten had been coming to her for haircuts since he was 14.

Next door, at Lee's Nail Salon, 30-year-old David Pham was putting the top coat of burgundy polish on a freshly manicured hand.

They both heard the cry: "Help! Help! My car's in the water and my grandson's in there!"

Pham, an immigrant from Vietnam, speaks little English. But terrified screams cross language barriers. He and Batten ran outside, where they met Pham's 28-year-old sister, Charlene, who was arriving for work.

The three ran to the water and jumped in.

Behind them were Clint Fountain, 23, and Daniel Tucker, 22, stock clerks at the Winn-Dixie supermarket. They were taking a break outside, so Fountain could smoke a cigarette, when they heard the screams; Fountain dropped his cigarette, and they ran.

Fountain didn't even stop to take off his black jeans and heavy work shoes before he dived in. The cold water was like a vise around his chest. It was hard to breathe. His head ached the instant he surfaced.

Tucker watched—but only for a moment.

"I can't swim real good," he told Ms. Cardona. "But somebody's gotta help that boy."

He waded slowly into the water and began dog-paddling toward the car, which was now sinking into 15 feet of water. He passed Pham and Batten, who had been overcome by the cold water and were heading for shore.

"Hey! Unlock the door! You hear me? Unlock the door!" Fountain screamed at Ryan. The water was rising to Ryan's waist as the boy frantically pulled at the child-proof locks.

Fountain's fists pounded against the glass.

* * *

Dick McClung, 32, a supervisor at Belk's department store, heard a commotion. He followed the cries and ran to the water.

His heart was pounding. There was a woman in a white shirt holding a hammer. No one knew where she came from.

She was just there. She raised it to throw it to the car.

"Don't! Don't throw it! You! Bring me the hammer!" Fountain screamed at McClung, who had already shed his sports coat. He gave no thought to his leather shoes, tie or pressed shirt and pants.

He dived in. The cold was paralyzing.

"Oh, Jesus. I'm not going to make it," he thought, halfway to the car.

"Come on! Come on!" Fountain screamed.

By now, the car was tipped nose first in the water, only the rear window and trunk visible. The water had reached Ryan's chest and was steadily rising.

McClung held the hammer out on his last two strokes to the car. Fountain leaned over and grabbed it.

Raising it above his head, Fountain brought the hammer down with every ounce of remaining strength, shattering the glass.

* * *

Cpl. Wendel Manning of the Georgia State Patrol heard the 911 dispatcher's frantic call, and his car was there in moments. In almost one motion, he got out, pulled off his gun belt and ran.

He saw Fountain smash the glass. He also saw Fountain's friend Tucker, struggling to stay afloat.

Manning jumped in, forgetting to remove his ankle holster. The frigid water made him gasp for breath. He couldn't seem to move.

In a panic, Tucker grabbed Manning and tried to climb on top of him, drag-ging them both under. Manning finally had to push Tucker away.

About the same time, passerby Charlie Mock had stopped to see what "all the ruckus was about." He saw a woman—Charlene Pham—floating face down. Mock jumped in and swam toward her.

He rolled her over, grabbed her by the neck and swam for shore. He was 15 feet from the bank when he felt something in the water. It was soft.

With his free hand, he reached down and grabbed. He came up with a handful of hair, then pulled Tucker's limp body to the surface.

By now, Manning had caught his breath. He grabbed Tucker and headed for shore. As they neared the bank, others waded in and pulled them to safety.

* * *

When the glass shattered, water poured into the car. Fountain and McClung—the Winn-Dixie clerk and the department store supervisor—pulled Ryan out. He clambered onto Fountain's back.

Fountain took three deep breaths and started to dog-paddle. McClung swam alongside. They were not two feet from the car when it sank.

"Man, you gotta take him. I can't do it," Fountain told McClung. He handed off the boy.

* * *

Their muscles ached. Every move was agony. Helping hands reached out to bring them ashore.

Paramedics pumped Daniel Tucker's chest for more than a minute before he spat up water and took a breath. He does not remember anything after wading into the water. He spent six days in the hospital with pneumonia.

Charlene Pham came to in the ambulance, unsure of much except that she had tried to help. Her brother rode with her.

Fountain and McClung walked past the paramedics, the firefighters, the onlookers. They headed for the Belk's store, where they grabbed clothes from the racks. They changed, shook hands and went back to work.

Manning drove back to the patrol post and changed clothes. Batten went home, his hair uncut.

"Nana! Nana!" Ryan screamed, wrestling free of the paramedics. He ran to his grandmother, arms outstretched, tears streaming down his face.

"My coloring book!"

The water had claimed only the book and the car.

Two days later, most of Ryan's rescuers came together again, this time for a picture. As Ryan clowned around with the hammer, they shook hands, laughed, retold their stories, and wondered at how heroism can visit average lives.

"You don't think," Fountain said. "You just do it."

Looking back, says Chelsea Carter, her AP career was going nowhere.

She had worked for a newspaper in California and then had gotten a temporary job—filling in for vacationing staffers—at the AP's bureau in Charleston, W.Va. She was there for eight months but never felt that she made much of an impression. Mostly, she says, she worked the broadcast wire, writing stories in a style suitable for television or radio. She rarely got out of the office.

Still, she managed to get a second temporary stint, this one in the Atlanta bureau. She was assigned to work three days and two overnights each week, and though she had her share of bylines, she didn't feel she had done anything that would induce the AP to hire her permanently when her time in Atlanta was up. She was resigned to finding another job at a newspaper.

Then Ryan Eschleman happened.

Bruce DeSilva, editor of AP Newsfeatures, had just visited the Atlanta bureau. With the fervor of an evangelist, he had promoted the idea of narrative storytelling.

DeSilva's visit had energized the Atlanta bureau. News editor Anne FitzHenry and assistant bureau chief David Simpson were eager to find a project that would lend itself to narrative treatment. On this Wednesday in February they thought they had found one.

The AP is a cooperative owned by its "members," the nation's newspapers and broadcast stations. As part of the cooperative agreement, the AP has the right to use news from the members. In the event of breaking news in an area where there is no AP office— say, a tornado occurs in an isolated part of the state—reporters for a local newspaper often get on the phone to the AP to share information they have gathered, at least until an AP reporter arrives.

For decades, AP editors combed through local newspapers, looking for interesting stories to rewrite for the wire. But in the age of computers, members often send the AP "electronic carbons," electronic copies of their stories. Early on Feb. 12, the Tifton Gazette sent the Atlanta bureau a carbon of its story about a small boy's rescue from a pond the day before. Tom Saladino, the day rewrite, made some phone calls and wrote up a short version to move on the wire that morning:

TIFTON, Ga. (AP)—Peggy Cardona could only listen to her 4-year-old grandson's screams as her car rolled down a grassy hill behind the Tifton Mall and plunged into a pond.

Nine different people responded in Tuesday morning's successful rescue of Ryan Eschleman, but two of them almost drowned as some of the rescuers had to be rescued from the icy water. Overnight temperatures in the south Georgia town had fallen into the 30s.

Ms. Cardona, 52, of Enigma, had forgotten to apply the emergency brake or place the car in gear because she was late for work as a hairstylist at a mall salon.

"I tried to stop the car and I fell out," Ms. Cardona said. "There was nobody behind the mall, and I ran to get help. If I had gone in with it, no one would have known we were there."

Devin Batton, Charlene Pham and David Pham were the first to respond. Clint Fountain and Daniel Tucker saw the commotion and arrived at the pond.

Fountain dove in and tried to break the back windshield of the car with his fist and foot. Tucker, who couldn't swim, jumped in to take a board to Fountain. Eventually Dick McClung ran from a store and saw Fountain, Tucker and Ms. Pham in the water.

McClung said that someone handed him a hammer and he jumped in to take it to Fountain.

Ms. Pham was on her way back to shore when the cold and the length of the swim took their toll. She passed out in the water.

Charlie Mock of Tifton, driving by, saw Ms. Pham floating facedown and jumped in to save her. While he was pulling her to shore, he bumped into something submerged in the water. He reached down and grabbed a handful of hair. It was Tucker.

"I guess I was just in the right place at the right time," Mock said. "If I was six inches further away, I wouldn't have touched him."

Mock was tiring when State Trooper Wendell Manning plunged into the water to help him.

Manning grabbed Tucker, who was not breathing, while Mock brought Ms. Pham, unconscious but with her eyes wide open, to the shore.

McClung reached the car at the middle of the pond and gave the hammer to Fountain, who smashed the glass and pulled young Ryan out of the car.

Fountain, weakened by the cold and tired from trying to smash the glass, made it halfway back before passing the child off to McClung. All three came ashore together with the help of Tifton Police Captain Buddy Dowdy.

Ryan, Ms. Pham and Tucker were taken to Tifton General Hospital.

Ryan was treated and released. Ms. Pham was listed in good condition Tuesday night. Tucker was listed in critical condition. Fountain was treated for cuts on his hand and released.

Ms. Cardona said she promised Fountain free haircuts for the rest of his life for saving her grandchild.

"There are heroes in Tifton," she said.

FitzHenry and Simpson felt this wasn't enough. There was a gripping story in the boy's rescue, but it would take much more reporting—and inspired writing—to make it happen. They obviously were more impressed with Carter than she knew; they believed the young reporter could get the story they wanted. Carter hadn't been at her desk for 20 minutes that morning when FitzHenry and Simpson told her to go home and get a change of clothes. She was going to Tifton.

FitzHenry gave Carter a copy of Saladino's story. She also gave her a copy of a book DeSilva had put together, a collection of the AP's best features. She told her to read a story by Julia Prodis; it would give her an idea of what she had to do. With that, Carter—a novice reporter with an intimidating assignment—was out the door.

"Remember to tell the story," FitzHenry yelled as she left. "Show me the story."

The trip to Tifton, 250 miles south of Atlanta, near the Florida border, took a little more than four hours. Carter and photographer Rick Feld took separate cars. On the way Feld used the phone in his car to track down Ryan's grandmother, Peggy Cardona, and tell her that they were coming. When they arrived at the beauty parlor where Cardona worked, she was there with her grandson.

First Cardona told the story from her point of view, while cutting a client's hair. Then it was Ryan's turn. "He was actually the toughest interview" of the entire assignment, Carter recalls. Children tend to give monosyllabic answers—"yes," "no," "I don't know"—and getting a child to warm up to a stranger is not an easy task. It takes patience. The icebreaker was Feld's camera; Ryan was fascinated by it. After a half-hour he told Carter how he screamed for his Nana. He demonstrated how he held on to the back seat.

Before they left, Cardona produced the hammer, which was found in the back seat of the car when the police pulled it from the water.

Cardona sent Carter next door to the Winn-Dixie to talk to Clint Fountain. Fountain related his story and then sent them to Belk's department store to talk to Dick McClung. The next stop was Lee's Nail Salon to interview

David Pham. Interviewing Pham was a challenge. He spoke little English, and Carter was able to piece together his story through hand gestures, a few English words and the help of someone who spoke Vietnamese.

Feld wanted to get a photograph of everybody together at the pond. Hours later they sat the cast of characters down in the lobby of the mall, and the rescuers again told their stories. This time each added to the others' accounts. "We did this again and again," Carter says. "I think they thought I was a little slow because I had them recount the story so many times. But with each recounting, more detail emerged.

"It's important to note that this is really where the sense of urgency came through because each person was telling his portion of the story and there would be interjections. People became animated and vocal about their roles."

Coincidentally, Carter was reading "The Corpse Had a Familiar Face," a book by Edna Buchanan. In it the novelist and Miami Herald crime reporter emphasizes the importance of detail. Again and again as she reported Ryan's story, Carter remembered Buchanan's advice: Always find out what was in the victim's pockets. Always look for visceral detail.

That detail emerged after Ryan, his grandmother and his rescuers had first given their bare-bones "I did this and then I did this" accounts. "It wasn't until the third or fourth time the group recounted the story that I started looking for details: color, touch, smell," Carter says.

There were three people with whom Carter was unable to talk: Daniel Tucker, the Winn-Dixie clerk, who was still in the hospital; Pham's sister, Charlene, who was ill; and passerby Charlie Mock, who worked and lived outside the area. Carter got Mock's account from the state patrol's report, where he was quoted; she depended on others involved in the story to tell her what Charlene Pham and Tucker had done.

Carter and Feld arranged to meet with some of the key players again the next day; Feld wanted more pictures. But that night they checked into the Holiday Inn. Catching her breath, Carter had her first opportunity to read the story in DeSilva's features book that FitzHenry had recommended.

"It just blew me away," Carter says.

Julia Prodis' story is the tale of three troubled kids: a girl and the two boys who loved her. Angry and alienated, they take off on a trip from North Carolina to Arkansas, stealing a car, gas and food along the way. When police lights flash in the rearview mirror, the boys kill themselves in a suicide pact; the girl, Jenny, survives. Her statement—obtained by Prodis—was the basis of an extraordinary story. This is how it began:

ROBBINSVILLE, N.C. (AP)— The trooper's blue lights flashed in the rearview mirror. Peck floored it, Josh grabbed the revolver, and Jenny, curled up beside him in the backseat, looked frantically out the back window.

They were far from home on this desolate Arkansas highway. It was the middle of the night, and the time had come for the best friends to fulfill their pact: If caught by police, the boys, just 15, and Jenny, 12, would commit suicide.

They had it all planned—or so they thought—days ago. Josh would shoot Jenny first. (She didn't have the guts to do it herself, and if she was going to die, she wanted Josh to do it.) He would shoot Peck next, then kill himself.

They were rocketing faster than 100 mph in their stolen Grand Prix, and the trooper was closing in. Just ahead, Peck saw a big rig blocking the only open lane in a construction zone.

They were trapped. It was time.

Peck slowed to a stop 20 feet behind the truck.

Josh cocked the gun, turned to Jenny, and looked deep into her green eyes.

"I love you," he said, and kissed her.

"Close your eyes."

How, Chelsea Carter asked, can I match that?

She went through her notes, which were scattered in two reporter's notebooks. She started ripping notes out of the books and putting them in some sort of chronological order. She used the king-size bed as a sorting table, moving left to right. She says, "I began with the notes on Cardona and the police report, noting the starting time, and then compiled the notes in order of the appearance of each key player. Meanwhile, I put together an outline of sorts in a notebook, noting where I was short of information and could clarify the next day."

She figured it out. From start to finish, from the moment Cardona pulled into the parking lot to the moment Tucker arrived at the hospital, the entire ordeal took 17 minutes.

On the drive home she thought the story through. By the time she pulled into her driveway, she had the basic framework—a chronology with little chapters to show the frantic moments that led to the boy's rescue—and an overline for the story: "17 Minutes: The Making of a Rescue."

The next day, when she arrived at work, she was installed in a small office and told to write. She closed the door. Two and a half hours later she had her first draft, about 2,000 words.

"Anne took it from me and started to read it. She made me sit in a chair in her office while she read it, which made me a little nervous. Then David stuck his head in, and she read the first five graphs. Both agreed it had to be changed—I needed to get the little boy and the fear in the lead. So I rewrote it, introducing the story from Ryan's perspective."

The Atlanta bureau is located in the Cable News Network complex; for the final edit, FitzHenry took Carter down into the atrium of the CNN Center, and there—away from the ringing phones, the televisions, and all the noise of the newsroom—they went through the story line by line, deciding what should stay and what should go. The final story was less than 1,500 words long.

To say that this story changed Chelsea Carter's life would be an understatement.

After the story was transmitted, she got a call at home. It was

Simpson, offering her a permanent job. She went out to a movie to celebrate.

The response to "17 Minutes" was phenomenal. Carter received more than 100 letters and messages from readers and colleagues. She went on to win the Associated Press Managing Editors Association Award for the best young AP reporter of the year. She moved on to the AP's New York City bureau and then was appointed correspondent in Orange County, Calif. Three years after the story was published, when she went to a writing workshop, other attendees approached her. Was she the one who wrote "the rescue story"?

All because she got the story and because she got it well.

"Timing," she says, "is everything."

18 Chasing a Fire

Charred Trees, Shattered Dreams: Chronology of a Wildfire

By DAVID FOSTER
Associated Press Writer

COYOTE GULCH, Mont. (AP)— Gusts of wind shake the pines in the yard. Lightning stabs down from the clouds. Good, think Sam and Kathryn Minor as they watch from their little house in the canyon. A little rain might take the edge off the heat.

But the rain never comes, and in 15 minutes the storm clouds pass.

Sam and Kathryn go to bed and think no more of it until morning, when they see—beyond the ridge, deep in the Bitterroot National Forest—two fat plumes of smoke.

* * *

The West is burning as it hasn't burned in 50 years.

Daily headlines recite the facts: This many million acres charred, that many homes destroyed. But what numbers can't convey is the dread and suffering every blaze brings. This is a day-by-day account of one canyon, one family and one of the wildest wildfires ever seen in the northern Rockies.

Experts say fire is an ecological necessity in the arid West, nature's way of cleaning house.

Yet ask those who live here, who breathe smoke for weeks, who watch flames dance in the blackened hills above their homes—if they still have homes—and they will tell you that when the forest burns, more is lost than the trees.

Sam and Kathryn Minor felt they'd found refuge when they moved last month to the foot of Coyote Gulch, 15 miles south of Darby in southwestern Montana.

Sam, especially, had seen hard times the last few years. Age 57 and disabled after two decades of roofing work in Las

---

Vegas, he'd weathered an ugly divorce and the deaths of his two teen-agers.

"Drugs—and more drugs," he explains tersely.

But then he found Kathryn, 48, and together they found a slice of paradise. They bought a small house with a big detached workshop, tucked away on two acres between Highway 93 and the east fork of the Bitterroot River.

It is quiet, private and just a stone's throw from the edge of the Bitterroot National Forest. Best of all, in this increasingly pricey part of Montana, they can afford it: $92,000 with $40,000 down.

They promise each other this will be the last move they'll ever make.

On July 26, they drive a U-Haul truck up to the workshop and fill it with two lives' worth of accumulation, both practical and sentimental: Christmas decorations passed down from Kathryn's grandmother. A china hutch. Bows and arrows. A futon couch. Plastic bags stuffed with clothes. Power tools. Glass figurines. An antique sewing machine. A microwave oven. A fire extinguisher.

They move some furniture and clothing into the house but leave 90 percent of their belongings in the workshop. No rush, they think. They have the rest of their lives to unpack.

* * *

The Minors aren't the only ones moving into the neighborhood. Six miles south on Highway 93, a tent camp of 500 firefighters is forming in a meadow to battle a blaze called the Maynard Fire, sparked by lightning July 22.

Hopes for any quick containment are dashed the evening of July 31. The dry-lightning storm that Sam and Kathryn see from their house starts fires through the mountains on either side of the Bitterroot Valley.

By the next morning, fire officials count 30 new smoke plumes. They dispatch ground crews and helicopters to dump water on the flames, 200 gallons at a time. They put out most, but six fires keep spreading, including the two the Minors had seen. They call them the Sula Complex and bring in reinforcements.

The next day, Aug. 2, Sam is plucking his guitar and Kathryn is singing along when a sheriff's deputy pulls up.

"I'm sorry to tell you this, but you have to evacuate," he says. "You have 10 minutes."

Sam and Kathryn grab food and underwear and corral the dogs—Bear, Bosco and Cinders—into the car and pickup truck. They drive seven miles up the road and spend two uneasy nights in the basement of friends.

By Friday, Aug. 4, things are looking up. Rain showers are cooling the flames. Highway 93 reopens, and Sam and Kathryn drive home to the canyon.

Firefighters tell them their house and workshop—both with metal roofs—look relatively safe. Four small pines grow near the workshop, but otherwise the two buildings are well away from trees and brush that can catch flying embers.

The closest fire is three miles and two ridges away.

By Saturday, despite the smoky skies and buzzing helicopters, things seem almost normal. The canyon is green and serene. The river bubbles past. "Wonderful," Kathryn recalls. "Idyllic."

* * *

By Sunday morning Chip Houde thinks his crews are making solid progress. The 46-year-old smoke jumper, part of a team flown in from Alaska, is responsible for 180 firefighters working two blazes across the highway from the Minors: the Gilbert Fire, 500 acres, and the Spade Fire, already 1,700 acres.

The Spade Fire is bumping down a hill north toward some houses; the Gilbert Fire is slowly chewing east through the forest toward Highway 2E.

In the morning cool, the fires creep along and Houde's crews can dig lines with hand tools right along the edges, one foot in the black, the other in unburned duff. Old logging roads provide ready-made firebreaks, and a bulldozer pushes fallen timber out of the way.

By 1 p.m., however, Houde grows concerned. The temperature is in the 90s, the humidity just 14 percent. The wind is picking up to 15 mph. And the flames lick higher.

Around 3:30 p.m., he sees the column of smoke from the Spade Fire, three miles to the northwest, bending toward the Gilbert Fire. He knows flying embers can start new fires up to half a mile from the main blaze, which would cut off their escape route.

He calls the sheriff's office and urges them to close Highway 93, then tells his crews to walk back to the buses. It is a calm, orderly retreat. In another half-hour, Houde says, it might not be.

Down at the Minors' house, the wind is swirling crazily, whistling through the trees, blowing ash through the yard.

About 4:30 p.m. Kathryn is cooking chicken-fried steaks when Houde shows up and advises them to evacuate.

Sam groans. "What, again?" He argues and asks if he can sign a waiver and stay.

Houde has no time. "We're leaving now," he tells them. "You should, too."

Sam and Kathryn take a look around. To the west, flames from the Maynard Fire are shooting up from behind the ridge. To the northwest, the Gilbert Fire is running down the hills toward the highway. To the east, yet another mass of flames—the Bear Fire—fills Coyote Gulch.

No more arguments.

"Hurry!" Kathryn yells at Sam. "We need to get out of here!"

Within minutes they are pulling out of the driveway, vehicles packed with the same bare essentials they'd taken the first time. The dogs are agitated; their owners are terrified.

On both sides of the highway flaming trees sizzle like slow-motion matches, in 30 seconds turning from green needles to black skeletons. Chunky embers whirl past their cars. The smoke is so thick they can see barely 50 yards ahead.

"Dante's inferno," Kathryn thinks.

"Unreal, like a movie," thinks Sam.

They arrive at the fire camp—a safe haven, in relative terms. Off-duty fire crews douse spot fires erupting around the meadow. Churning winds, powered by convection currents from the surrounding fires, lift a mess tent 50 feet into the air and slam it to the ground.

* * *

Back in the canyon Houde makes sure his crew gets out and tells every resident he can find to do the same. He stays behind to watch, driving from one already-blackened safe spot to another to avoid the roaring flames.

What he sees next is fire of an intensity he's witnessed only once before in 21 years of fighting fires. With winds gusting to 40 mph, flames boil 150 feet above tree tops. "This sounds like a cliche," Houde says, "but it really was a wall of flame."

The next day the camp's fire-behavior specialist also struggles for strong enough language to describe the blaze, calling it "the high end of extreme."

By 6:30 p.m., houses are burning, and the highway is littered with trees aflame and rocks loosened by fire.

By 8 p.m., as the sun dips toward the Bitterroot peaks and the blaze begins to cool, Houde orders crews back in to dig more lines and extinguish spot fires, hoping to save what structures remain. They work through the night and are replaced by fresh crews in the morning.

Sam Minor comes home Monday afternoon, hitching a ride with a National Guardsman patrolling the closed area. He sees the good and bad all at once: The house still stands, but the shop, 40 feet away, is gone.

His and Kathryn's life belongings are shriveled to a heap of black and gray. Sheets of roofing drape over the ruins like cooked lasagna.

All Sam can think of are Kathryn's boxes of Christmas decorations. Power tools and furniture can be replaced—not memories.

He kicks the smoldering rubble. He grabs a sheet of hot metal, and it leaves a painful welt on his forearm.

While the Minors' house and three others nearby survive, across the highway six foundations smolder where homes once stood. The houses are virtually vaporized, having burned so hot that only chimneys and thin layers of ash coating the cinder blocks remain.

In the few hours in which the fire blew up, the sheriff's office says, 52 homes in the forest were destroyed.

By Wednesday, Houde has rotated off the Bitterroot fires, moving on to blazes in eastern Oregon. The separate fires of the Sula Complex have merged into one big one: 78,000 acres and growing. Fire officials say they might burn until the snow flies in September.

At the canyon, Sam and Kathryn hunt for blessings to count. They've lost almost everything, but at least they have their house. "That's more than some," Sam says.

They don't have a signed insurance contract on the workshop, but Sam hopes the binder an insurance agent wrote up a few days before the blaze will cover them.

The rest of the week, they watch flames in the hills by night. By day, they walk the property, watching for hot spots, avoiding exertion to keep from inhaling too much smoke. Their scenic vista is now a view of ashen hills bristling with black poles.

Sam looks weary, beaten down. Every time he tries to describe what they've lost, tears well and he has to stop.

"This is devastating," he says, arms folded tight against his chest. "I don't know what we're going to do."

Then Kathryn shouts from the house: "Sam, the fire extinguisher! Now!"

A stump has flared up on the neighbors' property. Sam and Kathryn grab two extinguishers and a shovel and run, high-stepping over a wire fence. Sam kicks at the stump, sprays a white burst from the extinguisher and shovels dirt over the embers.

Sam is panting and red in the face. His feet feel as if his cowboy boots are on fire. Kathryn slumps against a blackened fence post, clutching her empty extinguisher.

Across the fence, in their yard, smoke starts billowing from another stump.

"Here we go again," Kathryn says with a sigh, and Sam trudges toward the burning stump, shovel in hand.

On a sizzling Monday morning in August the phone rings in David Foster's office in Olympia, Wash. New York is calling.

The fires in the West are heating up. His editor wants him to fly to Montana and help out the Helena bureau, where AP staffers have been cranking out daily fire stories for weeks. His mission will be to report the breaking news, do whatever the bureau needs—and while he's at it, look for a STORY.

Foster, the AP's Northwest regional reporter, knows what they want: real people, real drama, a compelling narrative that looks beyond the acres burned and homes destroyed.

And they want it by Thursday morning.

Foster pulls into Hamilton at 11 p.m., his adrenaline already rising from the fires he saw dancing in the hills as he drove in. The information office at the Bitter-root National Forest headquarters is still open, and he stops in.

He studies fire maps tacked to the wall and talks to a public information officer. The wind is calm and the fires are quiet, the PIO says. She gives him fire officials' phone numbers; he collects more numbers from the sheet on her desk when she leaves to make copies.

By 1 a.m. he's checked into the Super 8 Motel and is asleep in a room that smells, like the rest of this town, like a barbecued turkey.

*　*　*

Tuesday, 7 a.m.: At the information center again, Foster collects quotes and numbers about the wildfires. He calls them into Helena and then assesses his prospects for finding story material today.

There are three phases to these wildfires: the threat, when people in the fire's path pack up and leave home; chaos, with flames roaring and firefighters dashing; and finally, the aftermath, with burned-out residents sighing amid the rubble.

There is little chaos in evidence today. Northwest of Hamilton lies the threat, with fire looming near a housing development. Thirty miles south, in an area of burned homes, lies the aftermath.

Foster heads south. Along the way, in the small town of Darby, he stops at the Montana Cafe, thinking it a likely spot to find people who know what's going on. In the parking lot is a station wagon crammed with a hurried jumble of clothes, lamps and cases of soda. A fire refugee?

Sure enough. Inside the cafe, Judy Greene is just finishing her eggs. He asks her what the fire was like, and she describes driving out of the fire zone past neighbors' flattened homes, past pine trees burning like torches.

He spends a half-hour with her, asking the names of those neighbors and how he might get in touch with them. He also gets a number for the friend's house where she is staying in case he wants to reach her later.

Then he calls Helena with details of the interview, thinking it might provide some color for a sidebar. Instead, it becomes the lead of the day's main A-wire fire story, written by someone else but with Foster's name on top.

This is wonderful. It's only 8:30 a.m., and he's managed to toss a morsel into the maw of the spot-news monster. That'll hold it for a while. Barring a blowup of the fire, he's free to find a STORY.

He heads to the firefighters' camp south of Darby for a 9 a.m. briefing. Matter-of-factly, fire officials recite the acreage burned by the Sula Complex of blazes. Matter-of-factly, they explain that the wildfires displayed extreme fire behavior. They speak in lingo, generalities. They offer bureaucratically approved lessons on the ecological value of wildfire.

But what did the fire really look like? What did it sound like? What exactly do you mean by "extreme fire behavior"? They don't know. They weren't on the fire lines. They were back at camp, monitoring the blazes from afar.

There's no story here. Just information and strong signs that the Sula Complex is where Foster should go.

But no, they say, you can't go there. Highway 93 south is closed to all but fire personnel and homeowners who have signed waivers of liability, and even the homeowners can't get in without a sheriff's escort.

Instead, he gets a Forest Service tour of another burned-out area. A PIO issues him fire-retardant clothing, just like what the firefighters wear: yellow Nomex shirt, green pants, leather gloves, yellow hard hat, and a fire shelter in a box that clips onto his belt. He gets a 15-minute lesson on fire safety. He's heard it before, but he listens closely nonetheless.

Then they head up the road in a Forest Service rig. They see burned-out homes, a few fire-fighters doing mop-up, but not a single homeowner. After being driven around for three hours, he still has no material for his story.

But he does have that yellow shirt. When they return to the fire camp, the PIO lets him keep his fire-retardant clothes as long as he promises to return them when his tour of duty is over. Foster agrees and then zips out of camp in his rental car, a red sport-utility vehicle that some might say resembles a fire official's rig.

He heads south on Highway 93 and soon sees the roadblock ahead. Wedging the hard hat onto the dashboard, he rests his yellow-sleeved arm on the window frame. If the two National Guardsmen at the roadblock ask who he is, he will tell them, and they will no doubt make him turn around.

They don't ask. As Foster draws near them, he slows the car but does not stop. He nods knowingly and gives a little wave as he passes. They nod back, and he keeps rolling.

A few miles down the road he sees smoke curling up from the hillside pines. Here and there flames dance in the forest. He approaches the area near Coyote Gulch, where many of the 52 homes destroyed by fire over the weekend were located. He sees ashen house foundations with chimneys looming over them like tombstones.

There's still no story here. Just destruction. Nobody's home to tell him what happened. It's 3 p.m.

Then he sees a couple of homes still standing, surrounded by charred trees. In front of one there's a pile of black rubble. And there are people in the yard!

Foster pulls into the driveway. No, he's not a fire official, he explains. He's an Associated Press reporter. They seem relieved; they'd been told repeatedly by officials that they should evacuate, but they had decided to stick around.

Their names are Sam and Kathryn Minor.

He asks them what the fire was like for them, and for the next two hours they tell their story. Foster interrupts often, trolling for details. He knows that these people could be important to his story.

When they tell him they lost

everything in their workshop, he asks what was in it. Kathryn produces a handwritten list, and he copies down each item.

He doesn't want opinions or pithy quotes. He wants to picture exactly what they experienced, and he tells them so. He makes them start at the beginning, and he brings them back to chronological order when they stray from it, which they do frequently.

He listens for dialogue that they recall and makes sure to write it down between quotation marks in his notebook so that he'll be able to tell later that it's not just a paraphrase.

They tell the story in their own fashion, but Foster also asks a lot of questions: When the deputy arrived, what did he say? How did he say it? What did you say back? What were you thinking when the fire hit? If you were writing this story, how would you describe that moment to a reader? What were you eating for dinner that night? (He finds himself keenly interested in the answer, suddenly remembering that he hasn't eaten since breakfast.)

He asks for distances, ages, times, colors.

He asks the names of their dogs.

The interview is winding down. He makes them tell parts of the story again. It's also time for personal questions: How much did you pay for this place? How did your kids die?

Sam and Foster are sitting on a log in the front yard. Kathryn has disappeared into the house. Suddenly she's yelling at Sam to get the fire extinguisher.

Foster runs to his vehicle and grabs his camera, then joins them at a smoldering stump. He snaps pictures as they put out the fire. When they take a breather by the fence, he scribbles down their dialogue and actions.

He drives away happy. He has half a story now. It will chronicle the life of one fire, he decides, from the start to the present. Possible phrases, paragraphs and leads start to flicker in his mind.

Sam and Kathryn are essential to the story, but he needs more. He needs firefighters who were actually there. He drives south, toward the Sula fire camp.

Out on the road he changes back into street clothing and eats a power bar. Then he drives into camp and finds the information trailer. It's 6 p.m.

Two public information officers are there. They fill him in on the day-by-day growth of the fire. They give him acreage burned and numbers of bulldozers and helicopters. They point out landmarks on maps and give him photocopies of daily incident summaries dating back a week.

They're very helpful, but it's still not enough. These people weren't in the field. They don't know what the fire looked like, sounded like, smelled like. Foster is frustrated, and so are they, unable to answer his questions.

They call in Dave Dash, the operations commander for one of the fires within the Sula Complex. This is better. He knows where the fire crews went, what they did, what the weather was.

But Foster's still not getting what he wants. He asks: Can I talk to someone who was at the heart of the fire? One of the PIOs disappears and then comes back with Chip Houde.

Bingo! Houde is a branch director, in charge of several crews that worked the fire across the highway from Coyote Gulch. He was roaming the fire zone Sunday when the worst blaze hit. Best of all, he was the firefighter who told Sam and Kathryn Minor to evacuate that afternoon.

Foster asks him about that conversation. His account not only matches the Minors', it adds to it. He also tells Foster about the fire itself—one of the worst he's ever seen, he says.

Houde is not a perfect interview subject, by any means. He speaks in firefighter talk: generalities and macho understatement. If he was scared during the fire, he's not saying.

Foster has to pry good stuff out of this firefighter, and he's sure he's missing a lot. Hungry for details (not to mention dinner), he wishes he could interview Houde at a quiet restaurant instead of in this cramped trailer, with Houde's colleagues sitting nearby.

But that is not to be. Houde's exhausted, about to go off shift. Tomorrow he'll rotate off this fire to another assignment in Oregon.

They wrap up the interview, and Foster hits the road. He dawdles through the burned-out zone, hoping to find someone else at home, but there is no one.

He's back in Hamilton by 10 p.m., slouched in a diner next to the Super 8, devouring a hamburger and flipping through the three notebooks he's filled this day.

Yes. This will be enough, he concludes. He has a story.

He's asleep by midnight and awake again by 6 a.m. Wednesday, reading the news report on his laptop computer and calling fire officials to see what's up.

He calls Helena and asks if he can break away to write a feature for the Sunday papers. Another AP staffer is in Hamilton now, and the fires are not threatening inhabited areas. Go ahead with your story, he's told.

His motel-room bed soon is littered with notebooks, photocopies, topographic maps and pages torn from local newspapers. He makes a few follow-up phone calls and checks the AP for some facts (the archive, containing all national stories back to 1985, is accessible from any computer that logs onto the AP network). But 90 percent of the story is contained in his notebooks.

He writes all day and then all night.

He agonizes over the lead all morning and spends the evening filling in a chronology. At 4 a.m. he does push-ups to stay awake. He is ruthless, shaping and cutting his story; readers will never learn that Bosco is a Rottweiler, Bear is a blue heeler, and Cinders is a black poodle. Nor will they see the pitiful ceramic squirrel lying on its side in the ash of the Minors' workshop.

By 9 a.m. Thursday he has sent his story to New York. By noon, editor Julie Dunlap is on the phone, grilling Foster for details, stumping him only once or twice with questions he doesn't have the answers to in his notes. She has sliced 200 words from the story—painlessly, according to Foster.

At 12:48 p.m. the story is on the wire, and Foster falls onto the bed.

An hour later his cell phone rings. It's the Helena bureau. They want to know what Foster is planning for the next morning's newspapers.

19 The Tools of Investigative Work

For a long time investigative reporting and the AP went together like bananas and squid. The AP did breaking news, the AP did features, but the AP was not known for the kinds of investigative projects that have been a mainstay of American journalism since the Watergate era.

That has changed.

In recent years the AP has looked into safety problems at amusement parks. It has investigated the illegal employment of children in factories and fields. It has won a Pulitzer Prize for its examination of reports that American servicemen killed civilians at No Gun Ri in the Korean War.

"There's certainly a greater emphasis on what we call investigative reporting, although I've never really liked that phrase, because all reporting is investigative," says Lou Boccardi, the AP's president.

"It's a label for that front-page disclosure kind of story. There's vastly more of that than there was before. And mostly that's a good thing, as long as it's done responsibly and you are careful not to fall in love with a story and let it lead you astray and let your guard down."

The AP's stories are meticulously sourced and carefully reported. An in-depth look at the methods these reporters use would be the stuff of another book; from these examples, though, it is clear that three things are required of anybody who wants to do this kind of reporting:

- Fearlessness about asking unpleasant questions.

- The ability to organize complicated stories.
- A willingness to do hard work.

20 Investigations: A Mental Patient's Death

"Somebody Help Me . . . I'm Dying"

By BILL BASKERVILL
Associated Press Writer

PETERSBURG, Va. (AP)—Gloria Huntley lay alone and helpless, her breathing labored as she screamed and struggled against the leather belts that bound her spread-eagle to a bed in a state-run mental hospital.

"Client yelling and screaming . . . IM (intramuscular shot) given for agitation," is how Central State Hospital recorded her condition.

Fifteen minutes later: "Client continues to yell."

And finally: "Client complains of breathing difficulties. . . . Inhaler . . . given."

It was June 29, 1996, the end of a month in which Huntley, 31, had spent nearly 300 hours strapped down in solitary confinement, including two separate stretches of more than 110 hours— 4½ days straight.

Her latest offense, according to hospital records: falling to the floor on her way to lunch, refusing to cooperate, urinating on herself and screaming and yelling.

On the last day of her life, Huntley had complained to aides on the way to the dining room, "I can't walk, I can't walk," according to another patient.

"She collapsed in the hallway. They told us to step over her and keep walking," said the woman, who spoke on condition of anonymity because she said she feared retaliation by hospital officials.

"She was real, real sick. She said, 'Somebody help me, somebody help me, I'm dying, I'm dying.' "

She was right.

But staff members, mindful of the explosive temper that landed Huntley in the prisonlike Forensic Unit, took her back to the women's ward, placed her in the seclusion room and strapped down her arms and legs.

* * *

Born in Richmond on Oct. 20, 1964, Gloria "Sissie" Huntley was a "gladful, playful" child, "always into stuff," said her mother, Gloria Hobbs. "I had a hard time keeping up with her."

She was a tow-headed child with a wide, inquisitive smile. She loved to swim and dance and play with coloring books and baby dolls, said her mother.

Mary Holmes, Gloria's sister, remembered her as a 6-year-old attempting to free a puppy from a neighbor's fenced yard. She "had a spoon trying to dig up under the gate to get it out," Holmes said.

As she got a little older, Gloria enjoyed playing baseball with girlfriends, said Holmes, who was a year older than Gloria.

But she was hyperactive with severe reading and writing disabilities that caused social and academic problems in school.

"About 12 she started running away," said Mrs. Hobbs, who was bedridden with lupus at the time. "I don't know why."

It was probably the numerous disputes she had with her stepfather that forced Gloria to leave home, her sister said. "When she got in arguments with him she started running away. She hated authority."

She went to Central State for the first time at age 13 because she was a runaway. Hobbs regained custody shortly before her daughter turned 18.

About a year later, Gloria tried working as a hot dog vendor in downtown Richmond, but lasted only one day. She couldn't read well enough and didn't know how to multiply, said Jill Vansise, who has operated the stand for the past 14 years. "I thought she might be all right if she tried very hard and somebody was very patient with her, but she never showed up again," said Vansise.

Gloria hit the road again. She ended up in New Jersey, where she spent about five years in a state mental hospital before she was returned to Central State. Later, she ran off to North Carolina and was placed in a mental hospital there for 10 months. She was returned to Central State in 1992 so she could be closer to her family.

She was diagnosed with psychotic, mood and personality disorders that sometimes erupted in flashes of anger and violence. She was sent to the maximum-security Forensic Unit after attacking two staff members in another Central State building on July 5, 1995.

Her mother agreed that Gloria had a hair-trigger temper but said the outbursts occurred when she believed she or another patient had been wronged. "She would jump right in," Hobbs said.

*　*　*

Central State Hospital, a 127-year-old institution once called Central Lunatic Asylum, used restraints liberally as a therapeutic tool for Huntley's laundry list of mental disorders. Belting her arms and legs—and many times her chest as well—to a bed while she lay alone and stared at the ceiling was supposed to make her better.

The U.S. Justice Department is investigating patient treatment at Central State, including whether the hospital violated a federal law barring excessive use of restraints. Central State patient Derrick Wilson died in restraints in May 1993.

Mrs. Hobbs said her daughter told her she would be placed in restraints for no apparent reason. "She started crying and all and said, 'I ain't done nothing.' "

But Mrs. Hobbs said she had no idea how much time her daughter lay strapped to a bed. "It's a lot I'm hearing now I would never have imagined was going on."

Huntley's former psychiatrist and physician, Dr. Dimitrios Theodoridis, warned hospital officials a week after the July 5, 1995, attack on the staff that Huntley could die in restraints because she had asthma, epileptic seizures and a heart condition. He also appealed to staff members to follow his treatment plan of nurturing and encouraging Huntley. Instead, he wrote in a memo titled "Duty to Warn" that the staff became more menacing toward her.

Theodoridis threatened to remove himself as Huntley's doctor at that time, saying he could not be part of a disciplinary treatment program.

Shortly afterward, she was transferred to the Forensic Unit, which houses mental patients charged with crimes.

"One day I will get my life togetter (sic)," she wrote her mother after arriving in the Forensic Unit. "I hope you can see that before it is too late."

* * *

Mental health experts say Central State Hospital's use of restraints in Huntley's case was excessive and should not have been part of her treatment plan.

"Mechanical restraints have traditionally not been used for treatment simply because they are restrictive," said Dr. John R. Lion, a Baltimore psychiatrist who served on an American Psychiatric Association task force that studied seclusion and restraint.

Clarence J. Sundram, chairman of the New York State Commission on Quality Care for the Mentally Disabled, said he could not recall anyone in his state ever being held in restraints as long as Huntley had been during the last month of her life.

"It is highly, highly unusual," he said.

Associated Press reports about Huntley's case prompted Central State in March to stop using restraints as part of its treatment regimen and to require that nurses continuously watch patients in seclusion and restraints. Previously, an aide with no medical training checked every 15 minutes.

Huntley was left alone after a nurse gave her several puffs from an inhaler about 1:30 p.m. on June 29.

A half-hour later, patients received an urgent message to leave the ward, according to the Forensic Unit patient who witnessed the lunchtime incident.

"I walked past and so many were in the seclusion room where Gloria was that I couldn't see her," she said.

A registered nurse wrote: "Bluish tinge to entire face. No pulse or BP (blood pressure) . . . pupils fixed & dilated. Skin cold and clammy, body flacid. . . . No response to enterventions (sic)."

"Patients were crying and screaming and hollering," said the Forensic Unit patient. "They were saying, 'Gloria's dead! She's dead!' "

The state medical examiner said Huntley died from "acute and chronic myocarditis while in restraints." Myocarditis is an inflammation of the heart.

* * *

Hospital staff stuffed her meager belongings into a garbage bag and sent them out with her body.

The sum of her life at Central State: a hospital-issued yellow pajama bottom; a pair of worn-out gray pants with holes in them; a yellow T-shirt; a blue jacket; romance novels; a partially used tube of toothpaste and other toiletries; coloring books that perhaps bespoke ties with the happier days of childhood.

Huntley's meticulously folded final letter to her mother was postmarked June 28 and arrived the next day, about two hours after she had died. She thanked Mrs. Hobbs for sending some money and enclosed a Carmelite Friar prayer card seeking divine intervention during time of need.

The prayer reads in part, "O Holy Mary, Mother of God, Queen of Heaven and Earth, I humbly beseech you from the bottom of my heart to assist me in this my hour of urgent need."

It started, as so many stories do, with a phone call.

"I'm calling from a phone booth on Midlothian Turnpike," the caller told Bill Baskervill that Friday afternoon. "I have something very important to show you."

It was January 1997, a week after Baskervill first wrote that the U.S. Justice Department was investigating the death of a patient at Central State Hospital, a state-run psychiatric facility in Virginia. Authorities were looking into reports that Gloria Huntley had died in restraints; the state commissioner of mental health said nothing had been determined.

Baskervill's story had appeared in the Richmond Times-Dispatch. It caught the eye of one reader—even now, years later, Baskervill will not reveal her identity—and she said she needed to see him.

Baskervill was supervising the AP's Richmond bureau that day. After checking with his news editor, he took off for home, where he met the caller, a woman he did not know. She presented him with an eight-page memo written a year before Huntley's death by her doctor, Dimitrios Theodoridis, under the heading "Duty to Warn." Aides had repeatedly strapped Huntley down by her arms and legs and sometimes her waist to punish her, he complained. He cautioned hospital officials that his patient suffered from asthma, a heart condition and epilepsy, and if she was placed in restraints, she could die.

"It was explosive stuff," Baskervill recalls. He was supposed to be at the desk as the only staffer scheduled to work in the Richmond bureau the next day, but he was too excited to lay off the story; in between the local sports stories and weather reports, he set out to tell this troubled woman's tale.

*   *   *

Baskervill had worked for the AP for 30 years, since his discharge from the Army. He had not always specialized in investigative reporting; a quiet man, he is not Hollywood's idea of a dashing investigative reporter.

In fact, his first brush with what he calls "hard-edged reporting" came in 1990. He had written a couple of stories about David Hackworth, a former Army colonel who had been embittered by his experiences in

Vietnam and had lived in Australia for nearly two decades. Hackworth called Baskervill one day from Fort Bragg, N.C., a stop on a book-signing tour. "I have a hell of a story here. There's a master sergeant in the 82nd Airborne Division who's accused of war crimes in the Panama invasion," Hackworth said. "He hasn't talked to anybody, but he'll talk to you."

Baskervill went down to Fort Bragg, where he met Sgt. Roberto Bryan. "Don't tell my lawyer I'm talking to you," Bryan said. They met at a Taco Bell and then went to Bryan's house.

"He said, 'Listen to my phone, it's tapped.' I don't know whether it was tapped or not, but for three days we had to run around like this. He said, 'Here, you've got to check your car for bombs.' I said, 'You're kidding.' He said, 'No, let me show you how to do it.' So here I was for three days, checking my car for bombs and interviewing him and trying to talk to military commanders there at the 82nd Airborne.

"I've never felt more alive. I loved every minute of it."

A week later his bureau chief, Dorothy Abernathy, called him in and offered to make him the bureau's news editor. He accepted.

"Worst mistake I ever made," he says.

He tried to report while editing over the next four years, but it was no use. Finally, he gave up the management job and returned to reporting.

He has written about the uniforms American military men and women wore in Saudi Arabia and Kuwait during the Gulf War— uniforms that were uncomfortable because they were made of synthetic fabrics and did not breathe the way cotton does. He has written about faulty fire sprinkler systems and dangerous college dormitories. He has written about the long-term effects of a eugenics experiment in Virginia and about the Virginia Department of Minority Business Enterprise, which allowed a $300,000 program to assist minority businesses to languish for more than a year.

His work has won awards. It has forced changes in government, and it has changed lives. But he says these things matter little to him.

"I get awards. I accept them to be polite. But I'm not in the business for awards," Baskervill says.

"For me, the pleasure is in the reporting—the raw journalism of doing these stories. Some people would say, 'Well, Bill, you must get a lot of satisfaction out of helping these mentally ill people, or minorities, or ladies in prison, or college students.' Maybe I do, if I think about that, but not very much. I'm on to my next story. Sure, if they spend millions to help improve the public health system, that's fine. That's good. But I don't think about it, don't dwell on it. I want to do something new."

That something new might come in the form of a call from a source or a manila envelope pushed under his door. He saves every tip and checks out each one, though he estimates that only one in 10 becomes a story. "It's time-consuming, but it's a great feeling when you finally get something you can sink your teeth in; you know it's going to develop."

He keeps a file on every story. "I've got hundreds of them. Every story I've ever done, I've kept every note, every document, everything. They're all crowded in a little office here on the 13th floor of the 700 building here in Richmond. I brought some of

them home because I didn't have any more room."

Hard work is only part of the equation. Dealing with sources is another.

His sources, he says, "haven't given me documents for revenge or to make somebody look bad. I'm convinced they just want to do the right thing and were outraged by the way—in Gloria Huntley's case, the way patients were being treated. It's very rare for people to stand up like this. And in the case of my main source for Gloria Huntley's story, she faced not only professional risk but personal risk as well. Not that she could be hurt physically, but in her personal life.

"After a while, if you deal with someone for months or even years in one case, you become friends with them. And over the weeks or months you establish trust. That's the most important thing—trust," he says. "The source for Gloria Huntley and the mental health stories that got everything started—I haven't written anything about that for more than a year, but I still call and just chat. I've gone over their house and visited with them. When I first started doing the stories, I knew where they went to church, so I would meet them at church on Sundays."

If churchgoing helped forge a relationship, well, so be it. If nothing else, it pleased his wife.

*   *   *

The mental health stories were different from the others he had done. They were personal.

"In '95 I had a nasty case of depression myself. I don't usually broadcast that around, but I'm not ashamed of it," Baskervill says.

He got interested in the way the mentally ill were treated. He wrote a profile of a 10-year-old boy who battled depression. He wrote another story about the use of electroconvulsive treatment—shock therapy—for those who did not respond to any other treatment for depression.

Along the way he made friends in the psychiatric world. One day a source sought him out to report that the Justice Department was investigating the deaths of two patients at the state mental hospital, allegedly in restraints. "The work that I put in developing him as a source and other sources in the mental health community helped because they were going to

take it to the Washington Post, to the Times-Dispatch, or to us. And so they chose us because of the contacts I'd made and, I think, because I'd been open and honest about what I'd experienced myself." And that led to the call that produced the "Duty to Warn" memo.

To Baskervill this was the smoking gun, proof that patients at Central State were being mistreated—fatally so, at least in this case. But he needed more.

Who was Gloria Huntley? Nobody seemed to know, except that she was a 31-year-old woman who originally came from Richmond. On a hunch, Baskervill checked the files of the Times-Dispatch for the days after Huntley's death on June 16, 1996. And there he found it—Huntley's obituary, along with the names of her family members.

Baskervill had been trying to get Huntley's medical records but had hit a bureaucratic wall; under the law, patient confidentiality meant that only family members could see those documents. What he didn't know was that her family also had been trying to get the records for a year, but with no luck.

"I talked with the authorities many times, virtually pleading with them to give me their side of the story so it would be a balanced story. But they never did. They would just say 'no comment' and very rarely would elaborate or say anything else. For me, when they started doing that and stonewalling, it was like blood in the water for a shark. I loved it. It just made me work even harder."

On Valentine's Day in 1997 Baskervill accompanied Gloria Huntley's grandmother, mother, brother, sister and sister-in-law when they made a surprise visit to Central State to demand her records.

It was a tense scene. Baskervill told state officials that one way or another he was going to write a story: Either he was going to write a story about what was in those records or he was going to write a story about their refusal to turn over records to which this family was entitled.

Fifteen minutes passed while the state attorney general was consulted. And then Baskervill and Gloria Huntley's family got what they had come for.

They sat around a long table and pored through reams of paper. "Look at this," said Page Griggs, Huntley's sister-in-law. She had found daily reports that Huntley had been in restraints.

"I want to focus on the last several months of her life, to see what happened then," Baskervill said.

It was all there. This woman who suffered from heart disease, asthma and epilepsy, whose doctor had warned that she could die if she was placed in restraints, had been strapped down for 300 hours in the last month of her life, including two stretches of four and a half days straight.

A few days after Baskervill's story ran, the chairman of the state mental health board announced the creation of an independent commission to investigate whether patients' rights were being violated in state mental hospitals. Six months later the state commissioner of mental health resigned. Eventually the Justice Department issued a scathing report about patient abuse and death at Central State; along the way, one of Baskervill's sources regularly faxed federal authorities Baskervill's stories to guide their investigation.

He continued to do stories about state mental hospitals: about Skander Najar, who died of an untreated illness at Northern Virginia Mental Health Institute (half the doctors in the hospital were fired two months later). About Maura Patten, a patient at Western State Hospital who had severe respiratory disease and complained that she was dying. Two days later she was dead. But the hospital's director, citing patient confidentiality, wouldn't tell Baskervill anything.

"I knew which building Maura died in," Baskervill recalls. "So I drove over there after leaving the administration building. Some patients and staff were outside on the steps, and I asked if they knew Maura. Sure, they said, she lived on the second floor.

"So I strolled in. It is a public building, after all. The door to the second-floor stairs was unlocked, and so I went up. I walked into the ward and asked if anyone knew Maura's roommate. Turned out the person I asked WAS Maura's roommate. She told me she was in the bathroom when Maura died."

At about that point they threw Baskervill out of the hospital.

"You have to have a thick skin. It doesn't bother me to call up the governor's office or the state mental health commissioner or whoever I'm talking to and ask hard questions. If they dislike me because of it, so be it. I don't care. I don't worry about it; I don't give any more thought to it.

"I don't think it's a talent. It might be a pathology," he says, and laughs.

21 Investigations: All the Pretty Horses

Created to Save Horses, Program Sends Them to Their Doom

By MARTHA MENDOZA
Associated Press Writer

RENO, Nev. (AP)—A multimillion-dollar federal program created to save the lives of wild horses is instead channeling them by the thousands to slaughterhouses where they are chopped into cuts of meat.

Among those profiting from the slaughter are employees of the Bureau of Land Management, the federal agency that administers the program.

These are the conclusions of an Associated Press investigation of the U.S. Wild Horse and Burro Program, which has rounded up 165,000 animals and spent $250 million since it was created by Congress 25 years ago.

The program was intended to protect and manage wild horses on public lands, where they compete for resources with grazing cattle. The idea: Gather up excess horses and offer them to the public for adoption.

However, nothing in the law prevents the new owners from selling the horses to slaughterhouses once they take title to them. It is common for horses to go to slaughter when they grow old or fall lame, but nearly all former BLM horses sent to slaughterhouses are young and healthy, according to slaughterhouse operators.

Under the program's rules, anyone can adopt up to four horses per year, paying $125 for each healthy, government-vaccinated animal. If the adopters properly care for the horses for one year, they get legal title to them in the form of handsome BLM certificates bearing individual identification numbers that are freeze-branded into each horse's hide.

"We're working toward helping people develop pride in their horses," said Deb Harrington, a BLM spokeswoman

---

in Oklahoma. "These titles are suitable for framing."

Using freeze-brand numbers and computerized public records, the AP traced more than 57 BLM horses that have been sold to U.S. and Canadian slaughterhouses since September. Eighty percent of those horses were less than 10 years old and 25 percent were less than 5 years old. Ten years is not considered old for horses, which are often ridden well into their 20s.

At the Cavel West slaughterhouse in Redmond, Ore., for example, proprietor Pascal Derde pulled a sheaf of BLM certificates from a folder and explained that they were for horses he recently processed at his plant and sent to Belgium for human consumption.

Nearby, the carcass of a BLM horse dangled on a hook while butchers sliced the lean meat into packageable cuts.

"Killed on Friday, processed Monday, Thursday we load the truck and then it's flown to Europe," said Derde. "Monday it's sold in Belgium, Tuesday eaten, Wednesday it's back in the soil."

"The sad thing," said Pete Steele, a former BLM employee living in Montecello, Utah, "is you've got a bunch of wild horses rounded up and nobody wants them except for some folks who see there's some money to be made here."

Asked about the AP's findings, Tom Pogacnik, director of the BLM's $16 million-a-year Wild Horse and Burro Program, conceded that about 90 percent of the horses rounded up—thousands of horses each year—go to slaughter.

Has a program intended to save wild horses as a symbol of the American frontier evolved into a supply system for horse meat?

"I guess that's one way of looking at it," Pogacnik said. "Recognizing that we can't leave them out there, well, at some point the critters do have to come off the range."

Clifford Hansen, a former U.S. senator from Wyoming who introduced the bill to create the program, now wishes he could remove his name from the legislation.

"The law was intended to recognize the significance of wild horses and burros, but talk about a waste of public funds," said Hansen, now 84. "It's become the most ridiculous thing I ever heard of."

The government spends an average of $1,100 to round up, vaccinate, freeze brand, and adopt out a horse. Adopters pay $125 for each healthy horse, and can get lame or old horses for as little as $25, or even for free. After holding the horses for a year, the adopters are free to sell them for slaughter, typically receiving $700 per animal.

The government spends $1,100. The adopter can make $575 or more.

The sellers find no shortage of horse meat buyers. The demand for American horse meat has long been strong in Asia and Europe, where few share the common American compunction about eating the animal.

Today, demand is up in Europe because of fears of mad cow disease, said Luc Van Damme of Zele, Belgium, whose 100-year-old Velda horse meat business owns the Cavel West slaughterhouse.

According to the U.S. Census Bureau, 42 million pounds of horse meat were exported in 1995 at an average price of 62 cents per pound. In 1996 prices were up to 80 cents a pound and rising. France and Belgium were the biggest buyers, with others including Japan, Switzerland, Italy, Netherlands, Mexico, Canada, Sweden, New Zealand, Austria, Russia, Bahrain, Argentina and China.

While nothing in the law prevents sending an adopted horse to slaughter, government officials offer conflicting opinions whether it is legal or ethical for BLM officials to adopt and sell horses.

The Associated Press matched computer records of horse adoptions with a computerized list of federal employees and found that more than 200 current BLM employees have adopted more than 600 wild horses and burros.

Some of these employees, when contacted by the AP, could not account for the whereabouts of their animals. Others acknowledged some of their horses were sent to slaughterhouses.

In Rock Springs, Wyo., the BLM corrals are run by Victor McDarment, whose crew rounds up horses from open ranges in Wyoming, freeze brands them and arranges adoptions. It's a job that gives them access to thousands of horses.

According to BLM database records, McDarment adopted 16 horses. His estranged wife adopted nine. His children adopted at least six. His girlfriend adopted four. His ex-wife adopted one.

His co-workers in the corrals and their families adopted an additional 54.

Most of the horses they adopted were discounted from the normal $125 fee. Some were free. Discounting is allowed if a horse is injured, old, or otherwise unlikely to get adopted. Because he's in charge, McDarment decides if a horse should be discounted.

A discounted paint won a first prize for the McDarments at a national show last year. McDarment said the horse had been discounted because it had a leg injury.

On a sub-zero day, as steam rose from troughs where the wild horses drink, McDarment sat in a snow-covered BLM office with his managers and said he could not account for all the horses he adopted.

"I don't keep track," he said.

McDarment's estranged wife Carol McDarment, a hotel maid, said she never saw most of the horses adopted in her name.

"I just signed the forms and Vic drove them out," she said.

Some ended up with Dennis Gifford, a Lovell, Wyo., rancher and rodeo contractor who was barred from BLM horse adoptions because he was rounding up wild mustangs illegally and adding them to his private herds. According to court records, he has also been convicted of selling livestock without state brand inspections.

He said he has tried to breed McDarment's horses for bucking stock, and said he's sure some of McDarment's horses were slaughtered.

"They got to end up somewheres," Gifford said.

Some of McDarment's co-workers know where all their animals are. Jim Williams, for example, has leased land and is breeding burros from Arizona that he and his friends adopted. He sold additional horses at an auction to be used for roping cattle. He's hoping to make several thousand dollars a year off the foals.

"Of course, I want to make money off this," said Williams, stomping mud off his boots in a frozen corral.

"Is there anything wrong with that? It's legal, ain't it?" he said.

According to federal law, U.S. government employees are not allowed to use public office for private gain. The U.S. Office of Government Ethics said this means BLM workers may not participate in bureau programs that affect their financial interests.

But Gabriel Paone, the Department of the Interior's designated ethics official in Washington, D.C., said there is nothing wrong with BLM employees adopting wild horses, keeping them until they get the title, and then selling them for profit.

In fact, an internal BLM memo issued in November, 1995, "encourages employees to adopt and train wild horses and burros for their personal use."

"They're not doing this as public officials," Paone said. "They're doing this as private citizens."

"There's a real gray area in the way the law was written as to whether they're breaking the law or not," said Harrington, the BLM spokeswoman in Oklahoma.

So, the adoptions by BLM employees continue.

Michael Woods, a BLM range management specialist in Baker City, Ore., and his wife have adopted four horses since 1992 and sold them all.

One of his horses, a black mare with a star on her face, was rounded up as a foal from the high plains of Eastern Oregon in 1992. According to freeze brand numbers obtained by the AP from the Bouvry Exports Calgary Ltd. slaughterhouse in Fort Macleod, Alberta, Canada, the horse was killed in 1996.

Woods said the mare hurt her leg last year and wasn't working out as a riding horse, so he sold her.

"I assure you I didn't intend to sell her for slaughter," he said, "but the only one that was interested in her at the time was a buyer that takes horses to slaughter."

Woods would not say how much he was paid for the horse, which originally cost him the $125 adoption fee.

The federal government is conducting several reviews of the BLM's Wild Horse and Burro Program, with two audits and two reports to Congress expected to be completed in 1997.

"I welcome the scrutiny," said Pogacnik, who runs the program out of a converted warehouse in Reno, Nev. "It can only help."

Pognacik said he hopes the reports and audits will help him figure out what to do with the 15,600 wild horses and burros the bureau has identified as excess that are now roaming 10 Western states.

That's on top of more than 1,100 old geldings in an Oklahoma sanctuary that was slated to close years ago, and several thousand more horses awaiting adoption in placement centers across the country.

The BLM has failed to submit legally required biennial reports about the Wild Horse and Burro Program to Congress since 1992. An advisory council on wild horses and burros, required by law, has not convened since President Clinton first took office. BLM officials said it is because they are short of staff.

"We're here because we care about the critters," said Pogacnik. "They're a wonderful part of America, and we're here to protect them. Of course, we've got a ways to go."

Martha Mendoza had been working for the AP for just two weeks—and had been in New Mexico for just a week more—when she was sent out to cover a news conference. A group of animal rights activists claimed they had evidence that a federal program to protect wild horses was corrupt. There would be whistle-blowers, they promised.

The news conference was a fiasco. When Mendoza arrived, she was told by one of the organizers that she was a "fed" and would not be allowed in. She showed them her brand-new AP identification card, but they wouldn't believe her; the organizer pointed to Mendoza's green denim pants and said that if she wanted to infiltrate the news conference, the least she could do was change out of her uniform.

Mendoza was terrified. She had worked in newspapers and had taught school, but she was new at the AP and did not want to blow what appeared to be an easy assignment because of her jeans ("Which were the style at the time, I must point out"). She beseeched another organizer for help.

"But at that moment the real infiltrator—an Interior Department public relations agent pretending to be a radio reporter—was identified in the room," Mendoza says. "The animal rights activists grabbed her, and she began screaming at the top of her lungs. The alleged whistle-blowers, hiding somewhere in the building, heard the screaming and left." The whole thing dissolved into chaos.

Mendoza came away with a bunch of unsupported accusations and allegations, but her interest was piqued. In the months that followed she was assigned to work as a supervisor in the Albuquerque bureau. But when she came up for air, she would make some calls about the horses or read stories that had been written in the past about the Bureau of Land Management program.

But then, one evening, a letter was waiting for her in the office. It was from the public relations person—the one who was caught infiltrating the news conference—who said that the U.S. attorney had investigated the allegations about the Wild Horse and Burro Program and had decided that there was "evidence of wrongdoing," although no charges would be filed. Therefore, she said, there was no story, after all.

The words "evidence of wrong-doing" set off bells in Mendoza's mind. She called BLM employees and staffers; she called animal rights activists and horse slaughterhouses. Yes, she said, there was a story here.

She used the reporting she had done to draw up a proposal for an investigative project.

"Given a few weeks and using the Freedom of Information Act, I could get a database of all wild horses that had been rounded up by federal employees and were supposed to be adopted into nice homes," she said.

"A second database of federal employees could show me who works for the BLM. Run together, with the help of AP's computer whizzes, I could figure out which federal employees were adopting lots of wild horses. Then, with help from the slaughterhouses, I could learn which wild horses were being sold there instead of taken home to nibble grass in the pasture."

And that is what happened.

Barbara King, the AP's director of editorial training, says it is not surprising that Mendoza was able to pull off a project of this magnitude. Ask King to name the best reporters she has known in the course of her long career, and Martha Mendoza's is the first name that comes to mind.

"There is an intellectual curiosity; there's a sense of news," King says. "She is exhaustive in finding all the sources she can in her reporting. She is very conscious of the need for context and background."

Mendoza got the go-ahead to proceed with the story but couldn't do it immediately; a temporary replacement had to be found to do her job in Albuquerque.

But she also needed time to lay the groundwork to report the story. She had to file the Freedom of Information Act requests, she had to make travel arrangements, she had to get to call the slaughterhouse managers and get to know them so that she could see with her own eyes where the wild horses became food.

"I didn't know what I would find. The allegations could have been wrong, and my editors and I were clear my assignment was not to find impropriety but to learn whether the program was working as mandated by Congress," Mendoza says.

The actual reporting took a month, and it was a whirlwind. She had envisioned the story as a nuts-and-bolts report on a program that wasn't working as designed, but her editor in New York, Bob Port, knew that there was more to it than that; the horses held a romantic fascination that gave the story emotional impact.

Mendoza went out to the wild-horse roundup. It was "amazing, spectacular. Waves of these beautiful animals, tearing across the grasslands as a helicopter buzzed from behind. The cowboys—real, live cowboys—understood the animals, talked to them like children, moved them into trucks with patience and strength." It was cold; Mendoza spit, and her saliva froze in the air.

"The slaughterhouse was also fascinating. The horses were killed with startling speed and efficiency. The meat was prepared in sterile conditions, cold and clean. The dark red packages were shipped overseas to Belgium, France and elsewhere as dinner meat. And the slaughterhouse owner, a trained veterinarian, also showed compassion for the animals. He didn't want them to suffer. He was shocked that Americans find horse meat offensive but will happily eat other types of meat."

She tracked down men who worked for the program and were at the same time selling extra horses for slaughter for private gain. Some were brusque; when one retreated into an office to confer with his colleagues, Mendoza followed him and suggested that she should join the conversation.

Most were polite: "OK, perhaps they weren't exactly friendly when confronted with our evidence that the horses they adopted for $100 each had been turned around and sold for slaughter for about $800 each. But they were working for low wages in a program that simply wasn't working. There are simply more horses running wild on public lands than adopters who want them. And there isn't enough funding to adequately deal with them."

She had found them with the help of the database, which even provided a physical description of the horses that were sold and slaughtered—like the "black mare with a star on her face."

"While the color of the story came from the sights and sounds, the crux of the story came from the records," she says. She had filed sweeping requests for records, so sweeping that the Bureau of Land Management finally invited her to go through the files herself, under the watchful eye of a bureau official. She spent several days in an Arizona office, combing through records.

"We found workers selling their horses for slaughter. We found a program that had not filed annual reports in more than four years. We found a pattern of criminal investigations and convictions without resolution. And yet I found in this story what I found in all investigative projects—no bad guys, just a complicated mess.

"Yes, it's true that some people were probably breaking the law. And it's true that the program was not complying with its congressional mandate. But it is also true that the law enforcement division was unavailable to enforce the law and that without funds, the congressional mandate was impossible to carry out. The animal rights activists, furious over the horse slaughterhouses as a business, had their point—to them these were beautiful and thoughtful creatures, friends, in fact, being killed for meat.

"And yet the slaughterhouses also were doing a job. What else, in fact, can be done with unwanted horses? Who will care for them? And where could they all be buried when they die?"

Writing a story like this one is like negotiating a minefield. "We knew this story was controversial. We wanted to make sure we had it right," Mendoza says. She worked closely with her editors, writing and rewriting, and senior editors had to approve it. Facts were checked and rechecked.

As Port had predicted, the story made an enormous splash. The U.S. Senate investigated. The program director was replaced. The adoption rules were rewritten.

And there was one unexpected result: The slaughterhouse Mendoza had visited was burned down by animal rights advocates.

Mendoza moved on. After the success of this story, she took on new projects: stories about nuclear waste, child labor, a Pulitzer Prize-winning investigation of killings of civilians by American GIs during the Korean War.

And it all started with a news conference that went horribly wrong.

22 Investigations: Doctors and Tobacco

Healers Raising the "Killer Weed"

By ALLEN G. BREED
Associated Press Writer

RALEIGH, N.C. (AP)—Hundreds of doctors across the country own and profit from tons of tobacco, despite decades of health warnings, scolding from peers and in some cases their own ethical reservations.

They're family practitioners who warn teen-agers not to smoke, psychiatrists who treat addiction, oncologists who identify malignant tumors and surgeons who remove them.

One tobacco-owning doctor was a longtime regional medical director for the American Cancer Society. Another runs a public health department. A third writes a newspaper's health tips column.

Almost none smoke themselves.

"I won't smoke," says Stephen Jackson, an orthopedic surgeon in Paducah, Ky., who co-owns the government rights to grow 1,400 pounds of burley tobacco a year. "I mean, it will kill you."

All tell their patients not to smoke or chew tobacco.

"I get mad with them, fuss at them every day," says Richard Rush, a family practitioner from Conway, S.C., with more than 11,000 pounds of flue-cured tobacco allotted to his farm.

Nonetheless, they are among at least 760 doctors and other health care workers who own valuable federal tobacco-growing rights, known as allotments or quotas, according to a computer analysis by The Associated Press. They practice in 23 states, from Florida to Alaska, Massachusetts to California.

Some of the doctors own minuscule government rights, as little as 21 pounds annually; one in South Carolina has 932,000 pounds.

All told, these doctors control production of more than 7 million pounds of tobacco—enough to make 193 million packs of cigarettes a year. They also grow nearly 290,000 pounds of the varieties of leaf used in chewing tobacco and cigar wrappers.

At last year's sales prices, their leaf would be worth $13 million—although a large portion of that goes to family members, sharecroppers and those who lease much of the crop.

For professionals who have taken an oath not to do harm, those numbers are "shocking and disappointing," medical ethicist Arthur Caplan says.

"I think you just cannot argue that you're going to make money on the back of this obvious health menace," says Caplan, director of the Center for Bioethics at the University of Pennsylvania. "To own and farm and produce tobacco as a doctor, especially in small communities, sends a resoundingly wrong message."

The fact that many of these doctors grew up in those small communities is often their reason for being involved in tobacco. Even so, some are uneasy about it.

Dr. Edwin Norris has no doubt that a three-pack-a-day habit hastened his father's death at age 53 from coronary disease. And the Mountain City, Tenn., general practitioner and cosmetic surgeon has little doubt that tobacco produced under his 1,925-pound quota is harming other people's fathers.

"Even though it's legal," Norris says, "we're still responsible for some of the effects of it." His explanation for keeping the tobacco: Neighbors who actually raise it for him need the poundage to make a living.

Other physicians bought their farms as investments and acknowledge tobacco proceeds contribute to their wealth.

Although they may only get a nickel to 15 cents a pound for leasing their tobacco rights to farmers, quotas help pay mortgages and add to the land's assessed value. With talk in Washington about possible $8-a-pound federal tobacco buyouts some day, the leaf could constitute an even more valuable asset.

"I'm too greedy," George Burrus, a cardiovascular surgeon in Nashville, Tenn., says when asked about his decision to keep his 6,500-pound quota, even though he says he knows tobacco is "killing people." He clears about $4,000 a year from leasing his leaf.

"I don't worry about it enough to (sell out) since I don't feel like, say, the guy that's raising dope."

The AP identified these doctors by cross-checking a federal farm database with medical rosters from tobacco states. To verify matches, the AP contacted scores of physicians by telephone.

Some hung up when they heard the word "tobacco." Most who stayed on the line expressed ambivalence.

"Absolutely schizophrenic" is how Dr. William Grigsby described the notion of physicians growing tobacco.

"It's crazy, but I'll tell you why we do it," says the general surgeon from Kingsport, Tenn., who owns about 3,700 pounds of quota. "Almost the only doctors who raise tobacco have grown up on the farm and have kinfolks there."

One is Richard Calhoun. He was raised on a tobacco farm, and tobacco money helped put him through college and medical school.

On Wednesdays, when other doctors hit the golf course, Calhoun dons bib overalls and a baseball cap and drives a beat-up red flatbed truck around his mountainside farm in western North Carolina. He raises hay, cattle, Christmas trees and about 7,000 pounds of burley.

"Tobacco is a proud heritage for North Carolina," says Calhoun, who practices in Jefferson, near the Tennessee line. "I want to maintain that part of my heritage."

So while he lectures his three children—ages 9, 11, and 13—on the ills of smoking, he makes sure they help out on the farm.

"They're still young, but they know what it is to work in the dirt—and that this is actually a cash crop that can be grown for farm income."

He knows the links between the crop he grows and diseases he treats, from cancer to heart disease. Is that inconsistent?

"I do feel that tobacco is harmful to one's health," Calhoun replies. "But more importantly than that, I feel that, as citizens of the United States, we have the freedom of choice. And I don't think that governmental regulation should infringe upon one's ability to make choices in this regard."

Dr. Wendell Levi Jr. agrees. In 45 years as a thoracic surgeon he has removed cancer-ravaged lungs, but he has little sympathy for smokers.

"If they're stupid enough to smoke, that's (their) business, I suppose," says Levi, a Sumter, S.C., tobacco owner. "I've never had time to feel guilty about something like that."

Yes, he urges patients to quit smoking. "But it's not very effective."

But given the addictiveness of nicotine, quitting may not really be a choice, as even some tobacco-owning physicians acknowledge.

William Gause, a family practitioner in Columbia, S.C., says he quit cigars shortly before the U.S. surgeon general first warned against smoking's health hazards. But he knows how hard it is for others to stop.

"It's easier for me to get somebody off of, say, cocaine than it is to get them off of tobacco," Gause says.

Still, he says he never gave much thought to how his 3,000 pounds of allotment, passed down through the family for three generations, might be fueling that addiction.

"I've so many other things going right now," Gause says. "I've never really sat down to think about it. I may feel that way when I do—if I do."

Others have thought about it—a lot.

John Patterson, family practitioner and owner of a 900-pound quota in Irvine, Ky., has reached a moral bargain with himself.

He is the Kentucky Medical Association's liaison with two farm health groups and says the $230 a year he earns from tobacco pays for the gasoline he uses traveling the state, trying to help farmers diversify from burley.

"I think the question is: What is that doctor doing with that base?" Patterson says. "That is the way I've dealt with my ethical dilemma."

Elizabeth Ward feels as if she's a hostage of tobacco.

Ward, a physician's assistant in Wilmington, N.C., watched two years ago as her father slowly succumbed to smoking-related emphysema 15 years after he'd quit.

Around the same time, Ward bought a farm from her aunt because it adjoins her mother's property. The farmer who rents her mother's tobacco allotment says he can continue doing so only if he can also continue renting the tobacco on Ward's property.

"I'm a crusader against tobacco," Ward says between patients. "Every day, all day long, I talk to sick people, and a lot of their problems come from their bad habits—and bad habits I indirectly promote."

But her mother wants to live out her days on a working farm. So Ward keeps her connection to the industry and takes her $300 annual share of the tobacco lease money.

Many physicians make more than that on their tobacco.

Dr. Pickens Moyd answers several questions in a phone interview, but when the issue turns to how much the Hartsville, S.C., surgeon earns from his 2,000 pounds of tobacco, irritation creeps into his Southern accent.

"I'll tell you what," he tells a reporter. "You send me a check for half of what I'll lose, and I'll eat the other half. . . . YOU'RE not going to cough it up to stop this cigarette thing."

Frank Sessoms, a family practitioner in Pittsburgh who owns 2,200 pounds of allotment on a North Carolina farm that's been in his family for generations, also voices indignation. He's not part of some social problem, he says.

"I have a lot of patients, man, who always make excuses for themselves, for their behavior, whether it's alcohol, cocaine, tobacco, food," says Sessoms, one of 10 children of a steel mill worker. "I'm overweight and I ain't blaming Heinz because they make ketchup with sugar in it.

"I'm blaming me, because I'm just greedy as hell."

The income that medical oncologist Stanley Sides of Cape Girardeau, Mo., makes from 3,200 pounds of tobacco grown on his farm four hours east in Kentucky, he shares with a now-elderly neighbor who has helped tend the crop for 25 years.

But he resents being singled out as a physician.

"You could argue that the farmers in South and North Dakota that raise barley (for beer companies) are also contributing to a product that . . . hurts the lifestyle of many families. The issue is how far we take it."

"People leave paper trails when they thought there were none, and knowing where to look for those paper trails is half the battle," says Allen Breed, Southeast regional reporter for the AP.

The great thing about doctors and tobacco growers, says Breed, is that both have to have government permission to do what they do. It was the Lexington (Ky.) Herald-Leader's idea to look in the database of people who held the right to grow tobacco and match it against the database of Kentuckians who were licensed to practice medicine. But Breed took it one step further. He wanted to know how many doctors all across the country also were growing the leaf that is responsible for one of the nation's worst health problems.

It wasn't as easy as punching a few computer keys.

The U.S. Department of Agriculture had stalled for years but had finally released the database of tobacco holders. Breed contacted 12 states where the government administers tobacco price-support programs—Florida, Georgia, Indiana, Kentucky, Missouri, North Carolina, Ohio, South Carolina, Tennessee, Virginia, West Virginia and Wisconsin—and got lists of doctors licensed in those states.

About 300 of the names "matched perfectly, with middle initials and addresses all in alignment," he says. "But many of the doctors used different names and addresses in dealing with the USDA and the state medical board. Sometimes the name was just slightly different even though the hometown was the same."

Thus, it fell to Breed (with a little help from staffers in Knoxville, Tenn., and Louisville, Ky.) to call hundreds of doctors to make sure that they were also tobacco growers. And sometimes these were uncomfortable—even hostile— conversations.

Hardworking and tenacious, Breed was the perfect reporter for the job. He often calls people back several times after he interviews them "just to clear things up or make sure I heard things correctly."

"In fact," he says, "sometimes I worry that I call them back so much that I'm going to cause them to try to retract something. I pester the heck out of them."

He is a bear on accuracy. For example, "When I tape an interview, and yet I type it at the same time, I will go back, and if I'm missing the word 'the' or if I had the word 'the' instead of 'a,' I will go back and change that. Because I am so worried about getting anything wrong, that I'll even miss minuscule things like that. That's one of the reasons why I have always been against doctoring people's quotes to clean up grammar. I know that there are people . . . who feel that we shouldn't quote people directly using bad grammar, because it sort of makes them look bad. But I almost feel that if we change their quotes just to clean them up, we're basically saying that there's something wrong with them intrinsically."

To Breed, the calls to doctors were not only a way to ensure that the matches were made; he also could strike doctors from his list if they had stopped growing tobacco or recently had sold their land.

The calls took a month. Some of them were very short: "I basically just called the doctor's office and said, 'I've got an alternative number or address for Doctor So-and-So. Can I run that by you to see if he's the same person?' And

they would confirm or deny the address, and that way I had a match."

But others didn't want to give him an address. They'd ask, "Why do you want to know?" And he would have to say, "Well, I'm doing this to see if he owns tobacco."

In the course of those calls, when he talked to a doctor directly, he would ask the doctor if he was the person listed in the tobacco database: This was not the name of your father or son, right? Then he took the opportunity to ask the doctors some hard questions. How did they square their ownership of tobacco fields with the Hippocratic edict that they should do no harm?

"Just by bringing the topic up, I was sort of making a judgment call, that something was wrong with this," he says. But he understood that not all doctors were rich; some of these men and women had inherited the land. His own father was a doctor, and he knew there was an argument to be made that doctors should not be held to a higher standard.

In the end he allowed the doctors themselves to argue the issues in his story. There were those who hung up on him the instant he identified himself and explained why he was calling. But among those who were willing to talk, some felt guilty. Others did not. Many had not given the matter any thought, and others saw all the sides of the argument.

"So they basically told the story, and I was allowed to just be the conduit and remain somewhat aloof from any kind of a judgment call," he says.

Some calls led to discoveries. He talked to the husband of one South Carolina doctor. He suggested that Breed call another doctor in Florence, S.C. "This guy owns a million pounds of tobacco," the husband said. And it turned out to be true, and material for a sidebar. The former owned the tobacco under his and his wife's names and leased the rest.

"Some of the doctors were petrified," Breed says. "There was a cardiologist who gave me a great quote about how guilty he felt and how bad it would look. And then he called me back later and basically almost threatened me with a lawsuit if I released his name—(he claimed) that it would hurt his job. I let him off the hook

because although his quote was good, I didn't feel that it was worth it. I wasn't worried about a lawsuit. I just didn't feel that it was necessary to expose him to that situation if he was that worried about it. As a human being, I didn't want to expose him to undue grief just because I could.

"But I warned him. I said, 'The next reporter you don't say "off the record" to will not be as nice as I am and will not give you slack like this.' "

Breed was relieved of having to make some calls; computer expert Drew Sullivan went back into the database and found a field for honorifics or titles such as Dr. and M.D. But it is clear that to Breed, the many calls he did make were not a burden. He loves to report, and the database work was another weapon in his reporter's arsenal.

"With every story I find out about a new technique that was tantalizingly close to me on previous stories, and had I known about it, I would have had a much easier time. Like looking at tax records or looking at deeds. Deeds can tell you a number of things that you wouldn't normally think to look for. Looking at financial disclosures or Uniform Commercial Code listings in the county courthouse. Estate files. Things that will give you another avenue to explore, may give you another name to call."

Reporting, he says, is "frustratingly challenging. I hate being told that I can't have access to something. . . . I just like the challenge."

23 Using the Internet

Still Stuck in Vietnam, 25 Years Later

By JERRY SCHWARTZ
AP National Writer

The trouble is, he doesn't remember the names.

He arrived in Vietnam—the first time—in September 1966. He was 23 years old, a high school dropout from Paris, Texas. He was there about six months, came home with malaria, went back for a second tour in 1967.

Three decades later, Robert Blackburn is a retired professor. He lives in Missoula, Mont. He spends his days researching that long-ago war.

But the names. . . .

In the course of those two tours of Vietnam, he had seen many horrible things—"seen and done," he says. And more than 30 years later, he is afflicted by those memories in his dreams and in his waking hours.

He suffers, he says, from an "emotional numbness."

He suffers, he says, from remembering. And not remembering.

"I do not remember the name of any person I ever served with in Vietnam," he says quietly.

*   *   *

"The specter of Vietnam has been buried forever in the desert sands of the Arabian Peninsula," President George Bush proclaimed after the 1991 Persian Gulf War.

Except it wasn't.

On April 30, it will be 25 years since Saigon fell, 25 years since the last harrowing pictures of American helicopters setting off, desperate would-be refugees clinging to their landing gear.

Again and again over that time, we have been told that we are putting Vietnam where it belongs, in the dustbin of history, so we can become America again, proud and strong and sure of our moorings.

But again and again we are reminded

---

that we are still finding our way out of the Big Muddy. We see it in shattered lives, in our response to provocations overseas, in politics and relationships poisoned by the passions of days long ago.

In 1976, Jimmy Carter pledged if elected to pardon the draft evaders, "to bring about an end to the divisiveness that has occurred in our country as a result of the Vietnam War."

The pardon was one of his first acts in office. And nearly a quarter century later, Allen Comba, an attorney from Carteret, N.J., who served in Vietnam in 1970–71, still holds it against him.

"For me, it was a slap in the face of everyone who served," he says. One more thing: "I will tell you I'm not a big Jane Fonda fan."

Perhaps it is silly to think that we can divorce ourselves from the Vietnam War when we are still arguing over whether we should have fought it harder or not at all.

"The Vietnam War will be a major force in our lives until the entire baby boom generation dies out—and even after," says John Hellman, author of "American Myth and the Legacy of Vietnam."

It's like the Civil War, he says—the only period of American history that was more divisive.

At the end of the 19th century, Hellman says, there was a tacit agreement to honor the dead of both North and South, to lionize both Ulysses S. Grant and Robert E. Lee. We would put that war behind us, and enter the 20th century as a united people. The specter of the Civil War had been buried forever at San Juan Hill.

So why, in 2000, are we arguing about the rebel flag on the South Carolina statehouse?

* * *

"Tin soldiers and Nixon coming, we're finally on our own. This summer I hear the drumming, four dead in Ohio."

Just a few bars of an old song on a car radio, and Lou Szari is weeping. He hurtles back 30 years, to a warm, May day on "a really boring, really placid Midwestern campus."

He was a student teacher then. He was called to the principal's office, and told there was some trouble on campus. He got into his car and raced 15 miles, talking his way through military checkpoints and cutting through backyards and driveways.

When he got to Kent State, the campus was empty. His girlfriend was safe. But a protest against the war had ended grotesquely; four students—Allison Krause, Jeffrey Miller, Sandra Scheuer and William Schroeder—had been felled in a 13-second fusillade by Ohio National Guardsmen.

Liz Troshane saw it happen. She ran toward the fracas and yelled at the soldiers. "Suddenly I was surrounded. There were about a dozen of them pointing their rifles at me," she says.

In jail, she learned that Allison had died—Allison, the first person she had met when she arrived at school for orientation.

"Something died in me," she says.

More than 1,400 miles away Jay Hatcher was sitting in a freshman English class at University of New Mexico when his instructor arrived, wearing a black armband. There had been shootings at Kent State; a rally was scheduled for the plaza. Class dismissed.

Hatcher found himself in a mob that stormed the ROTC building. They broke a lock and trashed some files. "I got clobbered on the head by a guy in ROTC who was holding a baseball in his fist."

"At that point, my life changed," he says.

He never had supported the Vietnam War. It wasn't the same as the world wars. It seemed a waste of human life.

He became a hippie. He grew his hair down his back. A difficult relationship with his Army veteran father became "horrible, just horrible," to the point where they almost came to blows.

And he quit school, and thus lost his student draft deferment.

To escape the draft, he:

- Poked his arm with a needle so he would look like a junkie.
- Starved himself until he was down to 115 pounds.
- Complained of chronic colds, enlisted a psychiatrist, trumped up an arrest for blocking traffic during a demonstration.

None of it worked (the weight cutoff was 112). But in the end he was spared, he says, when the draft lottery was tied up in court.

In 1977, the hair came off, and he joined the Coast Guard. After more than 20 years, he retired and went back to school to become a history teacher. He grew his hair long again, grew a beard, pierced his ears. At the University of Wisconsin at Eau Claire, he is surrounded by kids who were not yet born on May 4, 1970, when Jay Hatcher became a radical.

Not long ago, he was sitting in a class discussion of the Vietnam War, listening to twentysomethings suggest that maybe the protesters were wrong, maybe the government had a point.

"Hey," he said. "These kids were your age, they were wearing T-shirts and jeans . . . and they turned upon them and shot them."

Hatcher, 48, speaks wistfully of the peace movement's failures.

"We were going to change the world," he says. "For the life of me, I wouldn't have thought that by the year 2000 we still would have civil rights problems and we still would have marijuana illegal and we would still be getting involved in petty little skirmishes overseas."

Liz Troshane still deems Vietnam "an illegal, illicit war." Once a member of Students for a Democratic Society, she became a teacher, saleswoman, addiction counselor—and now a financial adviser in Santa Cruz, Calif. She gave up on politics entirely after Kent State.

"What I gained was something called cynicism," she says.

When Lou Szari votes, he remembers the political duplicities he saw 30 years ago. And this 53-year-old professor at Virginia Commonwealth University tells his young daughters, "Never be in a crowd when they bring out the guns. The guns always win."

* * *

Steve Wozniak is 49, the same generation as Szari, Troshane and Hatcher. In the days of the Vietnam protests, he and his friend Steve Jobs—eventually, founders of Apple Computer—sold blue-box devices to college students who used them to make free (and illegal) phone calls.

Today he proclaims his faith in technology, not politics.

"I made a promise to myself a long time ago—back during Vietnam—not to be political," he says. "People act as if their candidate winning is a life and death matter. It's not. They think things will get better if their guy wins. It doesn't."

The cynicism bred by the Vietnam War has never dissipated. Instead, it has been deepened over the years by Watergate and all the other 'gates and by regular disclosures of the shortcomings of our leaders.

"Nixon and Johnson just lied through their teeth," says Robert Blackburn, the Vietnam vet. "People thought, 'Hey, our government lies to us. Our government can't always be trusted.' "

Meanwhile, the scorched-earth tactics of the war's opponents and their adversaries—"Hey, hey, LBJ, how many babies you kill today?" "America—love it or leave it"—opened a vein of political nastiness that persists.

Sometimes, you can still hear echoes of Vietnam venom. In 1998, when Barbra Streisand produced a movie about a shooting incident, Charlton Heston evoked Jane Fonda's wartime visit to Hanoi, reviling Streisand as "the Hanoi Jane of the Second Amendment."

Neither the left nor the right came out of Vietnam eager to order America's youth into battle. The conflicts have been brief and limited (Panama, Grenada, the Persian Gulf) or conducted from the air (Kosovo). In 1973, the year America officially left Vietnam, the draft ended and was replaced by a volunteer army.

Still, we battle over the draft—in the rearview mirror, through the candidacies of Bill Clinton and Dan Quayle and George W. Bush.

This year, for the first time, Americans were drawn to a candidate for national office in large part because of his Vietnam service.

But think about John McCain, says writer John Hellman. He was admired for his conduct as a prisoner, not as a fighter. It brings to mind the Rambo movie in which American soldiers were depicted as "innocent people who were victimized by the savage Vietnamese."

"It's the American hero we're rescuing, the American hero who has been unaccountably trapped and cannot get out," Hellman says.

Much like America itself.

* * *

"It's still fresh wounds, you know," says Mark Basinger.

He was just 17 months old when his father died; he has no memories of the man who left on a train in August 1966, and never came back.

His mother remembers, though. And

when she recalls Capt. Richard Louis Basinger, USMC, her tears flow.

"He was a breath of fresh air," Nelda Sue Basinger Ludwig begins.

They met in the train station in Lima, Ohio, in 1961; she was wearing a white dress, he was in his Naval Reserve uniform, bound for duty. She passed him a note, wishing him good luck. Two months later, he called her.

They married in 1964, when he graduated from Ohio Northern. They kissed goodbye at the same train station where they had met. Nine months later, on May 16, 1967, Nelda Sue opened her door to two Marines.

"I knew. They walked up the steps, and I asked, 'Is he dead?' And they said, 'Yes, he is.' "

She remembers the flag-draped coffin and her pride in the Marine Corps. "I acted the way Dick would have wanted me to, and that kept me together."

And she remembers how very much alone she felt.

"No one wanted to talk to me about it. They wanted me to get along with my life," she says.

So she did. She remarried in 1967 ("He's a wonderful man. . . . But when you've had the best, it's hard to settle"), had two more children, used her widow's benefits to help pay for a home for her new family.

Mark, meanwhile, watched the newscasts from Vietnam and thought, "That's where my dad died." His grandparents and aunts did not talk about Dick Basinger; the subject was too painful.

Mark wanted to know more. He has pieced together a Web site that pays tribute to his dad: his more than 350 helicopter combat missions. His journal entries, succinct and unemotional ("Emergency Recon Retraction and also one other recon insertion. Zone was 'hot.' No hits received").

An account of his father's death: "In the afternoon of May 12, 1967, Captain Richard Louis Basinger was killed in action when the UH-34D helicopter he was piloting (YZ-78) was hit by an enemy mortar round shortly after lifting out of a zone while on an emergency resupply mission to a Marine outpost at Con Thien."

"Captain Basinger was 24 years old"—11 years younger than the son who so desperately wants to connect with him.

In May, Mark will go to Vietnam. He will trace his father's steps. He will, he hopes, visit the spot where the helicopter crashed.

"I'm just trying to feel a part of him," Mark says.

But his mother says he need not go to Vietnam to do that.

"Look in the mirror," she says, "and you'll know your father."

* * *

There were 58,178 American deaths in Vietnam; their names are on a black wall in Washington (Richard Louis Basinger, Panel 19E, Row 92). But no one knows precisely how many children are left behind, or widows.

There are 2,043 Americans still missing in Southeast Asia. For purposes of survivors' benefits, all are presumed to have died more than 20 years ago.

But no one knows how many of those survivors still hold out hope for their loved ones; the status of the MIAs remains an obstacle to better relations with Vietnam, though four times that number remain missing from the Korean War, and 78,976 from World War II.

During the Vietnam War, 3,403,100 Americans served in Southeast Asia. No one knows how many are still struggling with the physical, mental or emotional fallout and the cold shoulder many of them received when they returned from this most unpopular of American wars.

Finally, "we got sick and tired of it" and demanded respect, says John Kinzinger, who heads the Ann Arbor, Mich., chapter of the Vietnam Veterans of America.

He was a radio operator in Vietnam in 1966 and 1967. Later he worked for Ford. Now retired, he gets together with a half dozen other Vietnam vets every Wednesday to eat breakfast at the Bomber Restaurant in Ypsilanti, take their 10 percent vet's discount, and chat about golf.

They don't talk about the war.

"That's asking to stir up emotions," he says.

* * *

Robert Blackburn often responds to e-mail from high school students who need information about Vietnam for class assignments, inevitably at the last minute.

How was life during the Vietnam War? "Dirty, terrifying, heartrending, intense joy at making such close friends, but ultimately just sad." Do you think the war was necessary? "No."

What can he tell them?

That Vietnam was weeks of tedium—monsoon rains, smells, heat, long hikes through tall elephant grass with 75 pounds on your back, leeches everywhere—punctuated by two- or three-day stretches of mayhem, the enemy outnumbering you, Marines falling around you?

That when you came back the first time, you tried to commit suicide unsuccessfully and then re-enlisted, hoping the Viet Cong would finish the job? But that you could not allow the young Marines under your command to die too, and so you soldiered on?

That you were shattered to hear that after you departed, the unit was wiped out—all of them killed or wounded by a bomb?

He will not tell them—or anyone—about the worst of Vietnam.

"There are some things I have to keep to myself," he says.

He has been in and out of VA hospitals. He blames both the end of his 29-year marriage and a heart attack on post-traumatic stress disorder; he is on 100 percent service-related disability, unable to teach.

Instead, he is researching all the American Vietnam casualties. He wants to explain every one—the circumstances, who died and how—so that their loved ones will know and perhaps put Vietnam behind them.

He has no illusions that it will do the same thing for him.

I was the editor of Penn State's student newspaper when the Vietnam War ended. Just young enough to miss the draft, I still carried a Selective Service card with a lottery number. Mine was 186.

When my editor asked me to write a story about the lingering effects of that war on America, I felt that I was both the right and the wrong reporter for the job. I knew the history—had LIVED the history—and could put it in context. But I was too steeped in Vietnam; I could not imagine what I could write about that era that had not been written.

We often are called upon to write anniversary pieces about long-ago crimes, disasters, events. Some regurgitate the facts of what happened, often entertainingly. Others take the main characters and bring them up-to-date, a kind of "where-are-they-now?" approach. I didn't want to do either kind of story. The facts of Vietnam—the people of the Vietnam War—have never left us. How could I inform readers about something they already knew by heart?

The very fact that Vietnam has never left us was the key. Over a couple of weeks, while working on other stories, I thought about the ways in which Vietnam was still part of the American landscape. It occurred to me that there were still many people, especially people in their 40s, 50s and 60s, for whom Vietnam was not a subject in the past tense. There were Vietnam vets, some of them troubled but most of them sliding toward senior citizenship uneventfully. There were the widows; young women when their husbands died, they had dropped out of view. And there were the protesters; their lives also were turned upside down by the war. Had they turned them rightside up again?

I didn't want this story to be a parade, a series of talking-head experts on Vietnam. Experts had their place, but I decided this story would be a series of miniprofiles of people who still lived with the reverberations of Vietnam, tied together with facts and quotes that would put them in context. These people are all around us, but the challenge was finding them and, more important, finding the right ones, the ones who had especially interesting and illuminating stories to tell.

If you were to stop people on the street, eventually you would find a veteran, or a widow, or someone with graying hair who had once stormed a draft board office. It might take a while. Alternatively, you could call veterans organizations or leftist groups. Or you could call people you have written to about Vietnam or others you know who have friends or contacts.

For this story, though, I chose to rely on a reporter's tool that did not exist when the last American choppers departed Saigon: the World Wide Web. This story was researched almost entirely on the Internet.

The benefits of finding sources on the Internet are simple. You will find people who have not previously told their stories in the mass media; you may learn something about them going in, at least enough so that you'll have an idea whether this might be a useful source. Often they are people who are eager to tell their stories; after all, they already have revealed themselves to some degree.

Robert Blackburn is an example. I found him with the aid of Google, a search engine. My search term was "Vietnam history," and among the first results was a site for teachers that included annotated links for the study of the Vietnam War. Looking down the list, I found this: "Dr. Robert M. Blackburn's website provides an excellent on-line discussion forum on the history of the Vietnam War. Robert Blackburn served two combat tours in Vietnam between 1966 and 1968 as a radio operator with the U.S. Marine Corps. He also holds a Ph.D. in American Political History that included a special study of America's involvement in the Vietnam War." Hmm. Sounded interesting. I went to his site and found a freewheeling discussion that had been going on for years. I also found indications that Blackburn still suffered because of his tours in Vietnam. I sent him an e-mail message, using an address from the site; he agreed to an interview and sent me his phone number.

But how would I know that Blackburn was what he said he was? The Web is infamous for charlatans: women who are really men, children who are really adults. I was able to find references to Blackburn's work in pieces by other historians, among them a review in a professional journal of a book he had written. The review had been written by a historian I recognized, a member of the faculty at Penn State. I was convinced Blackburn was the real thing.

The interview progressed from the general—Blackburn's insights into the war and its place in the American psyche—to questions about Blackburn's own experiences, his own psyche. He was living on disability connected to the war, he said, and he referred obliquely to that disability. I pressed him gently for details. There had been a heart attack and a broken marriage, and he blamed them on Vietnam. He had been in and out of Veterans Administration hospitals. Finally, he explained that he could not remember the name of a single person with whom he had served.

I could hardly breathe.

The interview with Nelda Sue Basinger Ludwig was no easier. I found her in a more roundabout way. My Google search for "Vietnam widow" turned up numerous mentions of Sally Griffis, a Vietnam widow who was doing a doctoral dissertation on the subject. I

e-mailed her, and after a time—she was in the middle of a move—we talked by telephone. She was a good background source, but she had told her story previously on television and in magazine articles. I wanted something new, and she provided the names and phone numbers or e-mail addresses of a half-dozen widows she knew.

One had become a counselor—very articulate, but she had written a book. Another had a terribly sad story to tell, full of loneliness. But she put me off repeatedly and finally decided that the pain was too great to revisit with an interview, even after all these years.

Nelda Sue Ludwig was willing. But minutes after I called she began to weep, and she cried through much of our interview. She insisted that I talk to her son, though he was just 17 months old when his father died and had no memories of him. But when I talked to him and saw the Web site he had created in his father's honor, I understood the void that Richard Louis Basinger had left in his son's life.

Veterans of the Vietnam protests are easy to find—all you have to do is cruise the many dis-

cussion groups devoted to the
1960s—but no single story
seemed to carry enough weight,
especially compared with Blackburn's and Ludwig's stories. It
was then that I tripped over a site
devoted to the shootings at Kent
State, and I realized that the 25th
anniversary of the end of the
Vietnam War almost coincided
with the 30th anniversary of the
killings on that Ohio campus.
Why not profile several people
who were touched by Kent
State?

I e-mailed several people who
had placed messages on an Internet memorial to the shootings.
Among them was Liz Troshane's:
"May 4, 1970, was a day that
changed the course of my life.
Almost 30 years later and I still
feel the pain as if it were yesterday. I will never forget the experience of that weekend, nor of
seeing my friends killed. Alison
was one of my closest friends and
I shall never forget her . . ."

Jay Hatcher's oral history, in
which he talked about how news
of Kent State led him to join the
antiwar movement, was posted on
the Kent State library's site. In it
he mentioned that he was at the
University of Wisconsin at Eau

Claire, working on a thesis on the
events of May 4, 1970; I looked at
that university's Web site and
found his phone number.

Lou Szari was also on the Kent
State library's site, but not volun-
tarily. The library had posted, as
PDF files, copies of all the reports
issued by investigators after the
shootings. I came across Szari's
name; he had been questioned in
connection with an attack on an
ROTC building in the days
before the shootings. His name
was unusual enough that I might
be able to track him down even
after 30 years. I logged on to
switchboard.com and searched
nationally for Louis Szari. There
was only one match.

I dialed the number. A man
picked up. Is this Louis Szari?
Yes. Is this the same Louis Szari
who attended Kent State at the
time of the shootings? A pause.

He was amazed. After all these
years, he had gotten a call out of
nowhere about Kent State.

Nearly everything in this story
can be traced to the Internet. I
learned about John Hellman's
book while going through a
library catalog on the Net; the
book was out of print, and so I
ordered it through an online used

book store and tracked Hellman through citations on the Web. The statistics were posted on the Veterans Affairs Web site. The quote from Steve Wozniak was from something he had written for Salon, an online magazine. John Kinzinger, the vet from Ann Arbor, was recommended by one of the widows I interviewed, who had been suggested by Sally

Griffis, whom I had found through the Web. Even the position of Richard Basinger's name on the Vietnam Memorial (Panel 19E, Row 92) was from the Web, in this case from a Virtual Wall on the Web. Only Allen Comba, the New Jersey veteran and lawyer, had no Web connection.

He had handled the closing on my house.

24 Changing Media and Media Careers

A reporter who started work at the AP in 1970 wrote with a typewriter and edited with a pencil. A reporter who started work in 1980 had to delve through file cabinets of yellowed clippings to unearth a history of jet crashes; there was no computerized archive. A reporter who started work in 1990 could not flip to a different screen and track down a Vietnam veteran on the World Wide Web.

The tools of reporting are always changing. It could be argued that none of these developments had the enormous effect of the invention of the telephone, which allowed reporters to collect information quickly, without leaving their desks. But even then, the telephone has never prevented reporters like George Esper from traveling long distances and ringing doorbells in pursuit of a story.

Reporting will always be reporting. It will always involve asking questions, collecting information, deciphering events.

But there will be changes, and some of those changes are apparent today. We are moving toward a time when the traditional distinctions between journalists who work with words, sound, still photography, and video are blurred, perhaps beyond all recognition.

"The buzzword right now is 'convergence,' and I think that's a relevant word to a would-be journalist at this stage," says Lou Boccardi, the AP's chief executive. "I think we are going to be reporting across several platforms. Maybe it's going to be the same person for at least some of the platforms. I think it WILL be the same person for at least some of the platforms."

Talk of convergence and platforms rankles some veteran reporters who envision having to juggle notebooks, microphones and video cameras and then prepare stories in all those media.

Jason Fields says they shouldn't worry. Perhaps he hasn't seen the future, but he has confidence that it will work.

As senior producer for special projects in the AP's multimedia department, Fields has played a major role in the creation of the WIRE, AP's Web site. He started his career as a reporter for a twice-weekly newspaper in Maryland; in 1994, when the Washington Post began its Internet enterprise, Digital Ink, he was an early hire. He didn't know a lot about computers, mostly what he had learned from playing around with video games. But he quickly embraced the possibilities of online journalism.

The WIRE mixes words, sound, and still and video pictures. Ted Anthony's story on the rise of English as a global language, for example, was illustrated with video of the pope speaking in English when he visited the Holy Land and recordings of radio voices from overseas.

Fields doubts that most reporters will be expected to shoot video. It's a specialized talent: "When I was at a tiny little paper, starting off, I took the pictures as well as writing the story. I think a lot of people went though that experience. Did that actually make me a qualified photographer? No."

But he does foresee a time when more reporters will be responsible for collecting sound: "You're used to having one of these tape recorders essentially to refresh your memory and make sure that quotes are verbatim and for other purposes like that. But not because you want to capture a quote so that you can put the person's voice out there. In the future, you may well be doing that as well," he says. "If you get an interview with the queen, it would be terrific not only to have the queen's own words in print but also to be able to listen to her inflection."

He likens it to the kind of work that is done on National Public Radio's "All Things Considered."

"In some ways it's like going back to a style of reporting that was more common 50 years ago. NPR does a lot of audio capture. They will have the sound. If they're doing an interview with the queen, you will hear the changing of the guard as the lead-in to the piece, and then you'll hear the clip-clop of someone's feet going down the hallway to illustrate the marble. And then they pull it together with the real sound of the interview.

"What we would love to have is reporters who are already on the scene and are willing to do more of what is commonly thought of as a broadcast job. We talk to some reporters who are very willing to do things like that, but others are very busy, and I'm not sure they want to do it."

At the very least Fields expects that reporters who have thought of themselves as lone wolves—solitary investigators armed with notebooks and their wits—will have to adjust to a more collaborative way of working, joining with others to produce multimedia presentations in much the way a TV crew works together to produce a piece for the six o'clock news.

"Lo and behold, they all have to work together," he says. "Which is terrifying to some people."

But Fields doesn't think this really changes the basic thrust of reporting: "You still have to get the facts. You still have to have to get the basic facts. . . . You still have to talk to everybody. You still have to try to find out everything.

"As a matter of fact, you may find that you're able to use more of what you reported, because there's an infinite news hole. And because of that space, you can include an interview that you'd have to leave out in print. Maybe that interview would be your audio, and it's not in your copy, it's supplementary to it. It almost works like footnotes to a certain extent. I don't think anyone's suggesting we put their notes up there, but you could have direct links to your sources, for example."

The reporters who are hired in the coming years, Fields says, will be those who are comfortable in different media and do not harbor prejudices against print or video or any other medium. Can he imagine a future in which the media do not converge and the Web is not a major force in news?

"Yes, I can," he says, deadpan. "But it's also the one after a nuclear war. We're all wearing these robes, and we're horribly disfigured. I have bad nightmares."

James M. Donna, the AP's vice president for human resources, points to newspapers that have set up television studios in their newsrooms: "A reporter will go out and write a story and then turn around and have to write a script because he's going to have to do it on TV in a minute. If we're going to survive, these kinds of things have to happen."

It is a good time to be a reporter, Donna says. There are many employers: newspapers and news services, radio and television stations and broadcast networks, dot-coms and magazines.

"Everybody's looking for content, and content is words," he says. "They're going to have to get it from an established source, like the AP, or they're going to have to create it themselves. Every Web site you have has got to have words on it, and somebody's got to write those words."

The U.S. Bureau of Labor Statistics says that the biggest job growth for reporters in the coming years will be online. There were 67,000 reporting jobs nationwide in 1998; six in 10 reporters worked at newspapers, three in 10 worked in radio and television, and the rest worked in magazines and news services.

Within the field, the new competition has meant that more people are moving from one job to another. "Now they're predicting that people are changing jobs five, seven times in their lifetime," Donna says. "And I see it—we have an awful lot of turnover. Our turnover four, five years ago was 13 percent. Now it's coming in at 18 percent. We're not alone. People are changing jobs."

Donna is seeing more job applicants with degrees in majors other than journalism—history, political science, economics—and more with advanced degrees: "I just got an application the other day from a woman who's got a medical degree and is looking to get into journalism."

Reporters' salaries have increased dramatically over the last 10 years, according to Donna, and will continue to increase "because we're going to be looking for more versatile people and I think the competition is going to be out there." There remains a wide range in compensation—from $15,000 for a new reporter starting out at a small-town paper to more than $100,000 for some veterans at major metropolitan dailies. And these people continue to earn less than they might as lawyers or executives in business.

"But one of the reasons people come into this business is the passion. And I see it every day," Donna says. "You get someone who probably could get into another profession and make a lot of money because they're obviously smart, and they're working in journalism, making fifty or sixty thousand dollars a year working nights and weekends.

"And when you ask, 'How is everything?' they say, 'It's a great story.'

" 'How's life in China?' 'How's life in Afghanistan?' 'How's life in Moscow?'

"They say, 'It's all right, but it's a great story.'

"And that's why they're there—because it's a great story. They feel compelled to tell the world what's going on. This is their calling."

About the Author

Jerry Schwartz is a national writer and editor for The Associated Press, and a veteran journalist with more than 20 years' experience working in the news service's New York headquarters. He has worked as special assignment editor, directing feature writers across the country. He has covered the courts, including the trial of subway avenger Bernhard Goetz; supervised election-night coverage of state and local elections; and traveled with the pope. He worked on the AP's special desk established to cover the Persian Gulf War and directed international coverage of the Y2K phenomenon. He has also taught feature writing at New York University and copyediting for the Dow Jones Newspaper Fund. Schwartz lives in Westfield, New Jersey.